# CAMBRIDGE LIBRARY COLLECTION

*Books of enduring scholarly value*

## Printing and Publishing History

The interface between authors and their readers is a fascinating subject in its own right, revealing a great deal about social attitudes, technological progress, aesthetic values, fashionable interests, political positions, economic constraints, and individual personalities. This part of the Cambridge Library Collection reissues classic studies in the area of printing and publishing history that shed light on developments in typography and book design, printing and binding, the rise and fall of publishing houses and periodicals, and the roles of authors and illustrators. It documents the ebb and flow of the book trade supplying a wide range of customers with products from almanacs to novels, bibles to erotica, and poetry to statistics.

## Wood-Engraving

William James Linton (1812–1897) was a wood-engraver, poet, prose writer and political activist, who first worked in London but emigrated to the United States in 1866. He began his wood-engraving apprenticeship at the age of sixteen under the well-known London engraver G. W. Bonner. Linton's mature work, championing the use of 'white lining' and favouring the use of horizontal engraved lines and creating tone by differing line thickness, continued in the tradition of Thomas Bewick (1753–1828), the founding figure of wood-engraving. The publication of this book in 1884 marked the culmination of Linton's career, though he continued to research and write on the subject. The manual, originally published in only five hundred copies, is beautifully illustrated with Linton's own engravings and is a rich source for anyone interested in the technical details as well as the historical development of this specialist craft.

# Wood-Engraving

*A Manual of Instruction*

William James Linton

CAMBRIDGE
UNIVERSITY PRESS

CAMBRIDGE UNIVERSITY PRESS

Cambridge, New York, Melbourne, Madrid, Cape Town, Singapore,
São Paolo, Delhi, Dubai, Tokyo

Published in the United States of America by Cambridge University Press, New York

www.cambridge.org
Information on this title: www.cambridge.org/9781108009089

© in this compilation Cambridge University Press 2009

This edition first published 1884
This digitally printed version 2009

ISBN 978-1-108-00908-9 Paperback

# WOOD-ENGRAVING

R. Branston, Sc.

# WOOD-ENGRAVING

A MANUAL OF INSTRUCTION

BY

W. J. LINTON

LONDON: GEORGE BELL AND SONS,

YORK STREET, COVENT GARDEN.

1884.

# PREFACE.

THE object of the following pages is to help toward forming a school of artist-engravers. With that end in view, it has seemed necessary to assert as absolutely as possible the true principles of Art (such of course as appear true to me), and to criticise unsparingly whatever I find antagonistic to these. In doing this I have cared rather to have my meaning clear than to leave any room for misunderstanding through fear of wounding the susceptibilities of those whose opinions might oppose my own. I believe that engravers will thank me for this plainness, seeing that all has been said in the interest of their art, and not without an earnest hope of benefiting them in the work before them.

W. J. LINTON.

LONDON, 1884.

# CONTENTS.

# ILLUSTRATIONS.

# WOOD-ENGRAVING.

## CHAPTER I.

### OF ENGRAVING IN RELIEF.

TO ENGRAVE, says Johnson, is *to picture by incisions.* The root of the word, writes Chatto, is to be found in the Greek γράφω (*grapho*), I cut: upon which he observes:—" From the circumstances of laws, in the early ages of Grecian history, being cut or engraved on wood, the word *grapho* came to be used in the sense of ' I sanction or pass a law;' and when, in the progress of society and the improvement of Art, letters, instead of being cut on wood, were indented by means of a skewer-shaped instrument (a ' stylus ') on wax spread on tablets of wood or ivory, or written by means of a pen or reed on papyrus or on parchment, the word *grapho*, which in its primitive meaning signified *to cut*, became expressive of writing generally. From *grapho* is derived the Latin *scribo*, I write ; and it is worthy of observation that *to scrive* (probably from *scribo*) signifies in our own language to cut numerals or other characters on timber with a tool called *a scrive*: the word thus passing, as it were, through a circle of various meanings, and in different languages, and at last returning to the original signification." [*Treatise on Wood-Engraving*, by Jackson and Chatto, 1838.]

Mr. Chatto's explanation will become clearer if, instead of cut *on* wood, &c., we say *cut in wood*, in wax, in timber: bearing in mind Johnson's definition—*to picture by incisions,*—to engrave (in French, *graver*) being really to grave, to cut a trench or a furrow, as with a spade or a plough, the cuts or incisions giving the lines of the writing or picture.

This is the ordinary process of engraving, no matter whether the engraving be in wood or metal : the subject (letters or pictorial lines) is seen cut *into* the material. The process and result are precisely the same, whether in a boy's name or initials cut on a tree, or on his school desk, or in the inscriptions (more mechanically exact) on tomb-stones, or (with more of art) in the monumental brasses of our churches and cathedrals. It is still the same process and corresponding result in the most delicate and elaborate engravings of steel or copper. The boy's desk-cutting, the lover's intertwined initials on a tree, the name of the disrespectful idler scratched into some wall or monument, —these all are, strictly speaking, engravings. We read them only in the hollows or incisions, soon perhaps to be effaced by the finger of Time wearing down the surface. So the names on tombstones become undecipherable ; and "Sacred to the memory" no longer lets us know of whom.

To preserve the name and effigy, as well as more clearly to expose them, in the costlier brass, the lines were filled in with black, in which may have originated the idea of prints,—the method of printing from the incised lines of a copper or steel plate being, as in the brass monument, to fill in the lines with black, not hard (as when merely to show the subject), but of soft ink, which (the surface first cleaned) by pressure could be transferred to paper, and the impressions multiplied. Whether *engravings* (using the word in its present more confined meaning of "*prints*") were so suggested, or not, what has been said may suffice to explain the use and method of incised lines, and how the same are available for prints.

In all this is no explanation of ENGRAVING IN RELIEF, which at first sight appears almost like a contradictory term, or a confusion of differing methods. By engravings in relief, let it be first said, we understand engravings in which the surface is printed, instead of the incised lines or parts. Such surface-printing is the necessity and the characteristic of wood-engraving, the very opposite of copper, in so far as the printing is concerned. Even though the process of printing copper-plates might have been taught by that filling-in of metal work for the mere sake of clearer perception of lines or figures, the first printing from surfaces would be suggested altogether independently of that, and so much earlier that there can be no possibility of our saying when. Anyone pressing a dirty finger on a white wall might perceive the fact of an impression, a print, if not too forcibly pressed, from only the surface of his finger, only the more prominent lines of the skin appearing. Between such perception and the invention and use of some rude stamp, the distance need not be great.

Such rude stamps were the precursors of what is now
known as ENGRAVING ON WOOD. And now
the usual term *on wood* will be rightly applied : all of our early wood-engraving being
of the character of this finger-mark. Though
produced by cutting (every cut an incision),
nevertheless it was not the cuts, the incisions, which
were to represent the writing or the drawing, but the
parts of the wood left on the original surface, that is to
say, in relief. And for this reason : the earliest prints
of the sort were designed by artists who, having learned
that there was such a thing as printing—taking impressions (as from the finger) by simple direct pressure or by
slower rubbing (which of the two processes they used does
not concern us here), were desirous of having their designs
multiplied without the necessity of repeated copying by
hand. Their usual habit of drawing upon paper would be in
black ; it would be almost a matter of course to draw in the
same way upon the plank of wood to be engraved. Simply
to have cut their lines *into the wood* would have given their

drawing in white upon black. In metal, as
has been before said, the ink can be rubbed
into the lines, and so *they only* will appear
black, the surface having been wiped clean
without taking the ink from the incisions.
In wood this is not possible, simply because the surface of
the wood absorbs the ink, and can not be wiped sufficiently
clean. Artists, then, drawing in black on the white or
light wood, wanted these black lines printed. We can
hardly call it invention—the seeing that it was as easy to
cut away all the wood, except the drawn lines, as to incise
the lines themselves. The former process, indeed, would

be easier for the unskilled hand of a mechanic, who would
have the lines he would leave on the surface always before
him, whereas in cutting out the drawn lines he would be
continually losing his guides. It has been supposed that
the early draughtsmen on wood engraved their own drawings. It may have been so at first. But it is not at all
likely ; it is barely possible (taking note of the vast
quantity of engraving executed even in the very early
days) that they could have had time to do it ; the work
also was wholly mechanical, so that any careful lad was
able for the performance.

We will conclude then that the designer drew (or it
may sometimes have been that an inferior artist drew for
him), with pen or brush upon the wood, a few simple bold
lines at first ; and it was the business of the engraver
carefully to cut away all the wood round these lines, so
cleanly and exactly that the drawing, to the very shape of
each line, should be preserved in its integrity, and that the
white wood should be cut away—that is, lowered—sufficiently to prevent it from taking the ink with which the
surface lines were to be blacked for the impression. An
" engraving " so produced is, it will be seen, not an engraving *of incisions,* but an engraving *of the relief.* For the
designer, this was an advantage. The pencil, or pen, or
brush, being more easily used than the graver, he could
more quickly make a drawing than he could engrave the
same in metal ; the material also was cheaper ; and there
was the further advantage, that the wood could be printed
with type (the wood planed to type-height), a considerable
economy in the production of book-work. This, however,
is beside our immediate consideration, which is only to
make clearly understood what " *engraving in relief* " for

surface-printing is, as distinguished from what should alone be called *incised engraving*, in accordance with Dr. Johnson's definition.

From the above, without further explanation, it might appear that wood-engraving, being all surface-printed, is scarcely to be called an art, at best but a less or more skilful mechanical leaving and preservation on the surface of the lines drawn by an artist. But it has already been shown that lines, as in metal, *can be* incised or cut in the wood; and, of course, with as much artistic ability and value, only that such lines in surface-printing would appear white. There is accordingly in later wood-engraving a combination of black lines (left on the surface) and white lines (incised), distinguishing the best modern work altogether from the only mechanical rendering of early times. This will be fully explained and illustrated further on. Enough here, if the reader perfectly understands what is *engraving in relief* for surface-printing.

Of SURFACE-PRINTING it is well remarked by Mr. Chatto that impressions from wood-engravings " are obtained by the *on*-pression of the paper against the prominent lines (the higher lines left on the surface), while impressions from copper-plates are obtained by the *in*-pression of the paper into the hollowed (incised) ones." In consequence of this difference in the process, the ink-lines communicated to the paper from a copper-plate appear prominent when viewed direct, while the lines impressed on the paper from a wood-engraving are indented in the front of the print and appear raised, embossed, on the back.

## CHAPTER II.

UR Manual of Wood Engraving may be not unacceptably prefaced with some brief account of the history of the art in its early days.

It must be utterly impossible even to conjecture when letters or characters were first cut into wood, or when they were first cut in relief for the purpose of stamping. Some blocks in relief seem to have been used for stamping bricks in old Babylon,—bricks baked or hardened in the sun having been indented with characters in their previous soft state. These bricks, about twelve inches square, can be seen in the British Museum. In the Museum also may be seen some ancient Egyptian stamps, brought from Thebes, with incised characters; and also a brass stamp of Roman time, engraved in relief, with the word LAR upon it, reversed as for printing. These specimens may be sufficient to prove antiquity.

It has also been claimed that the Chinese employed the

art of wood-engraving for books so early as the reign of We-Wing, 1120 years before the Christian era; and engraving *in* metal (copper, brass, silver, and gold) was certainly practised from a very remote period. We find it mentioned in the Bible, Aholiab and Bezaleel ornamenting the dress of Aaron: " They made the plate of the holy crown of pure gold, and wrote upon it a writing, like *the engraving of a signet,—*Holiness to the Lord." (*Exodus* xxxix. 30.) Engraved metal plates have been found in the coffins of Egyptian mummies. In India, long before our era, records of the transfer of lands were engraved in copper. Homer and Hesiod seem to have known of engraving. In the Imperial Library at Vienna is an engraved plate, some Roman police ordinance of 200 years A.C.; and Dr. Willshire gives, from Fabretti, an inscription from a bronze plate used (under a law of Constantine) to be worn on the collars of slaves in lieu of their being branded, as had been the custom. Engraving on or in wood, for many purposes, was possibly as old as engraving in metal. We may pass from these antiques, to come down to what is better known.

We may also pass lightly over the incredible story of the Two Cunii, given by Papillon, a French wood-engraver and writer on engraving of the eighteenth century. In his *Historical and Practical Treatise on Engraving in Wood,* 1766, he relates that he had once seen a book (size nine inches by six) containing " The Chivalrous Deeds, in figures, of the great and magnanimous Macedonian King, the courageous and valiant Alexander," which book " by us Alexander Alberic Cunio, knight, and Isabella Cunio, twin brother and sister," was " first reduced, imagined, and attempted to be executed in relief with a little knife on blocks of wood joined and smoothed by this learned and beloved sister, continued and finished together at Ravenna, after eight pictures of our designing, painted six times the size here represented ; cut, explained in verse, and thus marked (printed) on paper to multiply their number, and to enable us to present them, as a token of friendship and affection, to our relatives and friends.  This was done and finished, the age of each being only sixteen years." The date of this precious performance was fixed between 1285 and 1287 ; but the only authority for its existence is Papillon's account, professed to be written by him at the time of his seeing it ; his memorandum, however, was lost for thirty-five years.

It is certain, nevertheless, though Papillon's story (perhaps believed by him, the invention of a man not always in his right mind) affords no support to the position, that wood-engraving was used for taking impressions on paper or parchment, ink being applied to the surface lines, as early as the Cunii date : Chatto says—" in attesting documents in the thirteenth and fourteenth centuries." 'Toward the end of the fourteenth and about the beginning of the fifteenth century, he thinks it was employed for the outlines (before colouring by hand or stenciling) of cards, which, first brought from the East into Italy, somewhere about 1350, had in the course of a few years come into common use and formed a considerable branch of industry in France and Germany.  The term *Form-schneider* (figure-cutter), the German wood-engraver proper of the present day, then first used to distinguish the engraver of figures or superior subjects from the mere engraver and colourer of cards, does not, however, occur with any certainty until 1449, when it is found in the town books of Nuremberg.

By then the *Form-schneiders* had become a numerous body ;
and, though thus distinguished from the *Brief-malers*, or
card-colourers, we find them long after occasionally employed on similar subjects (the Brief-malers sometimes

*A Form-schneider at work.*

From Jost Ammon's " ARTS AND TRADES," 1564.

engraving figures) and forming together one single guild
or fellowship.  [*Treatise* by Chatto.]

Our business here is with the Form-schneiders.   Their
earliest, and, for a long while, their chief work seems to
have been the production of what may be called pictorial

tracts, single sheets of saints and martyrs, and later, of
more important Scripture subjects, at first the work of
monks in the convents, afterwards ordered and issued by
the City Corporations, as shown by the public registers of
Ulm, Nuremberg, Augsburg, &c. These single or " fly "
sheets of all sizes, generally small, but sometimes very
large (larger than two pages of the *Illustrated London
News*), served, writes Dr. Willshire, " as a great source of
religious instruction among the common people. To such
as could not read, and to them who could, but to whom
access to manuscripts of religious character was difficult,
these rude figures of the holy saints and martyrs, these
rough memorials of the Cross and Passion, attached to
which were often pious ejaculations and short prayers,
served the purpose of recalling to mind many of the lead-
ing Christian doctrines of the times, and the bright examples set by the heroes and heroines of the Christian
faith. The single figures of saints, and especially the
xylographic productions [xylo-graphy—wood-engraving]
to be presently mentioned as 'block-books,' served, in
conformity with a precept of St. Gregory, to assist the re-
collection of those who had heard the Scriptures read or
were themselves reading them, and to refresh the memory
of the catechist, whose teachings could be prompted as his
eyes passed over the symbolic illustrations. The chief
purpose was, in fact, a continuation of that which from
the time of Gregory the Great (A.D. 540-604) until now,
has been authorized by the Church, viz., the instruction
of the less literate by pictorial representations. On fast
days the Lazarists, and other religious orders, who were
accustomed to nurse the sick, carried in the streets large
wax candles, richly ornamented, and distributed to the

children Helgen [1] and wood-engravings illuminated with
brilliant colours, representing sacred subjects."

On these early fly-sheets there is neither name or mark
of engraver, nor date. Our earliest dated wood-engraving
was long considered to be a " Saint Christopher," an impression of which, coloured and much damaged, is in the
possession of Earl Spencer. It bears the date of 1423 ;
and was found pasted in the cover of a manuscript book
in the Chartreuse convent of Buxheim, near Memmingen,
in Suabia,—one of the most ancient convents in Germany.
The size of the *engraving*, a simple outline coloured by
hand or stencil, is 11½ inches in height and 8⅛ inches in
width. The subject is Saint Christopher, supporting himself with a palm tree as he carries the infant Jesus on his
shoulder, across a river,—the saint and child occupying
nearly the whole of the picture. Other smaller figures,
with Chinese absence of perspective, so much smaller as
to bear no proportionate relation whatever to the saint,
appear in such space as he has left unoccupied. On the
far bank of the river a kneeling hermit holds up a lantern;
a little in front of him a rabbit is coming out of a hole ;
and on the bank the saint has left is a mill with water-
wheel, and a man leaning against an ass which has a sack
on its back. Behind, on a road uphill, a man carries

---

[1] " Wood-cuts of sacred subjects were known to the common people
of Suabia and the adjacent districts by the name of *Helgen* or *Helglein*,
a corruption of *Heiligen* (Saints), a word which in course of time they
used to signify prints generally. In France the same kind of cuts, probably stencil-coloured, were called *dominos*, the affinity of which name
with the German *helgen* is obvious. The word *domino* was subsequently
used as a name for coloured or marbled paper, and the makers of such
paper, as well as the engravers and colourers of wood-cuts, were called
dominotiers." [Chatto, p. 45.]

another sack, going towards a house in "the distance."
All these smaller figures are of the same size, without any
reference to their position in the picture. The mere outline engraving is of rudest cutting, but, no doubt, was
coloured attractively. At the foot of the cut are two lines
of Latin, signifying that every day the likeness (this picture, of course) of St. Christopher is looked upon, the
beholder need not be afraid of any fearful death.

The claim of this St. Christopher to be the earliest
dated wood-cut has been within the last few years disputed,
in favour of a print said to bear the date of 1418, now in
the Royal Library at Brussels. This Brussels engraving
is a representation of the Virgin Mother (in a palisaded
garden) seated between two palm-trees, with crown and
nimbus, and holding the Child Jesus naked in her lap.
St. Catharine sits on her right hand, St. Barbara on the
left ; in front are St. Dorothy and St. Margaret. Over
the heads of the group hover three angels with wreaths ;
and on the gate of the palisade in front appears the date
M.CCC o XVIII. The circle in the centre is supposed to be a
nail (one of several) fastening a transverse bar of the gate,
and hence has arisen a contention that it has displaced L,
the sign of fifty, which would date the engraving fifty years
later. In the photograph (like the St. Christopher, the
print has been coloured) published at Brussels with
official sanction, this nail is not so clear as absolutely to
preclude the possibility of some tampering with the inscription. The drawing of the two prints gives also occasion for artistic dispute ; while the style of engraving,
in both very rude and poor, in no way helps toward a
solution of the difficulty. After all, the five years difference is of little importance. "Earliest known *dated*" is

far from implying that no earlier work had been *done.* We do know that such engravings on wood were rife even before 1400; and the establishment of an earliest dated work, unless earlier than that, is a question for the antiquary rather than the engraver.

"The next step," writes Chatto, "in the process of wood-engraving, subsequent to the production of single cuts such as the St. Christopher, in which letters are sparingly introduced, was the application of the art to the production of those works which are known to bibliographers by the name of BLOCK-BOOKS; the most celebrated of which are the *Apocalypsis seu Historia Sancti Johannis* [the Apocalypse or History of Saint John], the *Historia Virginis ex Cantico Canticorum* [the History of the Virgin from the Song of Songs], and the *Biblia Pauperum* [*Predicatorum*—the Book of the Poor Preachers]. The first is a history, pictorial and literal, of the life and revelations of St. John the Evangelist, derived in part from the traditions of the Church, but chiefly from the book of *Revelation ;* the second is a similar history of the Virgin, as it is supposed to be typified in the *Song of Solomon*, and the third consists of subjects representing some of the most important passages in the Old and New Testament, with texts either explaining the subject or enforcing the example of duty which it may afford. With the above the *Speculum Humanæ Salvationis* [the Mirror of Human Salvation] is usually, though improperly, classed : as the whole of the text, in that which is most certainly the first edition, is printed from moveable metal types. In the others the explanatory matter is engraved on wood, on the same block with the subject to which it refers " [CHATTO, p. 58]. The three first of these, Chatto thinks, might have appeared between 1430 and 1450. "That the *Speculum*, the text of which in the first edition was printed from metal types, should be printed before 1460, is in the highest degree improbable."

The *Apocalypse* (a copy is in the King's Library at the British Museum—a thin folio in modern binding, wanting two pages) consisted, when perfect, of fifty woodcuts, pictorial subjects, with explanatory text cut on the same block, one line or two or three lines divided from the picture by a single line instead of being placed under it. The slightly varying size of the pages is about ten and a half inches in height by seven and a half in width. Of these wood-cuts the most are divided into two compartments, each compartment containing a separate subject. In the upper portion of the first page St. John is preaching to a group of three men and a woman, the text informing us (in Latin) that *Drusiana and others are by him converted from their idols.* In the lower portion, in a sort of chapel, St. John is baptizing a very small Drusiana who stands naked in a font. Outside the chapel are six armed men apparently about to break their way in ; above their heads a text, stating them to be idolators watching the proceedings within. This one description may be sufficient for characterizing all. The cuts are in simple outline, the cutting clean, but not remarkable even for mechanical excellence. Chatto supposes the drawings to be the work of some Byzantine artist, driven from Greece by the Turkish invasion ; but the cutting by an engraver or engravers of the Netherlands or Germany. There is nothing to indicate which.

The *History of the Virgin* (this early block-book is not to be confounded with the History of the Virgin by

Dürer) is a small folio of sixteen leaves, printed in dark brown, on one side only, with two subjects on the page. There are two editions of this : the first supposed to have been engraved in Germany, the second in Holland. The designs of this book are very graceful, and there is some beginning of shadowing, but the cutting is of the rudest workmanship.

Of the *Book of the Poor Preachers* there are several editions. That in the King's Library at the British Museum is a small folio of forty leaves, printed in light brown, and on one side only. On each leaf are four portraits, of prophets or saints, two at top, and two at bottom, with text on each side and also upon scrolls. The centre of the page is divided into three compartments, each occupied by a subject from the Old or New Testament, the outer subjects in some way corresponding with or pictorially elucidating the subject in the middle. As, for instance, in page 14, where the middle picture is the Temptation of Christ by Satan, and the two supporting pictures are the Temptation of Eve, and Esau selling his birthright. There is a large amount of engraved text upon these blocks ; and the letters as well as the pictures are very rudely cut. Mr. Chatto takes the engraving to be Dutch or Flemish work rather than German.

The *Speculum,* or *Mirror of Human Salvation,* though no more remarkable than the preceding block-books for any peculiarity of cutting (all of them very rude and mechanically poor), may deserve notice here as having been engraved after the introduction of moveable types for printing ; one edition having the text in such types, another partly in moveable types and partly engraved on the block. Its date is supposed to be about 1480. Other Block-Books

of the same period need not be noticed here : they are all
of the same character, rude cuttings by unskilled or careless hands, such as might be cut by any boy of the present
time from a pen-and-ink drawing on a plank.

A book of *Fables*, printed by Pfister at Bamberg in 1461,
a small folio of twenty-eight leaves, appears to have been
the first book printed with types and wood-cuts, and there-
after it did not take long to establish the general applica-
bility of wood-cuts for books. The *Meditations of John of
Turrecremata*, in 1467, and a German *Bible* with cuts, 1477,
are notable as beginnings. The practice soon became usual
throughout Germany and the Netherlands. In England
Caxton brought out his *Game and Playe of the Chesse*, 1476,
with cuts. There are wood-cuts also in the *Golden Legend*,
1483, the *Fables of Æsop*, 1484, Chaucer's *Canterbury Tales*,
and other books of his printing : all coarse and poor enough,
but noticeable in the history of our art. At Ulm, in 1482,
we have the first instance of a map engraved on wood.
In 1486 appeared *Breydenbach's Travels*, a Latin edition,
printed by Erhard Renwick at Mentz, with folded engravings, views of Venice, Corfu, &c., that of Venice (upon
several pieces of wood, the impressions pasted together)
measuring five feet in length by about ten inches in height.
But what is more noticeable in this book is that in the
frontispiece the wood-cutter has had for the first time to
attempt the cutting of cross lines: a difficulty escaped in
all previous engraving. This frontispiece has an admirably
drawn figure of " St. Catherine," or perhaps the personifi-
cation of the city of Mentz, standing between two coats of
arms with rich scroll-work, and with grouped boys and
scroll-work above. In this cut we first notice the skill of
the form-schneider (yet, perhaps, but mechanical) in the

clear, sound, delicate lines, fine, sometimes crossed, an intelligent and evidently fair rendering of the artist's drawing.  The *Nuremberg Chronicle*, printed at Nuremberg in
1493, may be mentioned, not as equal to the *Travels* in the
engraver's work, but on account of its numerous engravings, executed under the superintendence of William Pley-
denwurff and of Michael Wolgemuth (the master of Dürer),
who has been wrongly supposed to have engraved them.
About the same date, or a little later, appeared in Italy
the *Hypnerotomachia Poliphili* (the Contention of Imagination and Love, by a general Lover), a book perhaps not too
highly praised for its designs, but for the engraving of
which there is little to be said, even on the score of
mechanical skill.

And here it may be pertinent to notice the confusion, in
all writings upon engraving, of *the design and the cutting.*
A drawing is strong, that is, it is drawn with broad and
vigorous lines of pen or brush ; straightway the engraver,
who merely cut away the plain wood outside the lines, is
complimented upon *his* boldness, breadth, and vigour,
without any consideration whether he has really been
true in his work or not.  Another cut has none but thin
lines in it ; and the critic exclaims, "How delicately engraved !" when the delicacy was only in the drawing.
Well-drawn or ill-drawn, the engraver's work is well done
only if he has been faithful to his drawing, if he has closely
preserved the lines laid down for him.  If he has been
true to his drawing, strong or delicate, he has done well.
If not true, not well. Similar confusion is made in judging
of the comparative age of these old wood-cuts. That a cut
was poorly or rudely done is no proof of its age.  The
wood-cutter could engrave as badly, that is, there have

been engravers as unskilful, in later days as in the earlier.
And even weakness and brokenness of lines may *sometimes*
only mean that the wood-cut has been much worn or un-
fortunately battered out of its pristine soundness. In
truth, until the close of the fifteenth century, the time of
Albert Dürer, we can find but few cuts, in the vast multitude done, which show anything more than such mechanical
dexterity as we might expect from any carver's or joiner's
apprentice after two or three or half-a-dozen trials.

A great engraver, indeed, was Albert—or Albrecht
Dürer, a great engraver in copper,—great in that as in his
painting. Great also for his designs, drawn, I suppose, by
himself upon the wood. But at the date of his first work,
engraving on wood had become extensively practised.
There was no need then for his hand-work in cutting,
even setting aside the easily to be shown impossibility of
his having had time to cut only a small portion of the designs known to be his. And it may be remarked that,
however skilful his hand might be in the use of the graver
in copper, the altogether different and unaccustomed work
of cutting with a knife would certainly not have been done
by him so well as by one used to it. The very excellence
(clean and exact rendering of line) would rather point to
the skilled mechanic as its doer: the better the work *as
engraving*, the less likely (and the remark applies to other
painters or draughtsmen credited with engraving their
own drawings on wood)—the less likely that he had any
hand in it. More truly is he called " the greatest pro-
moter " of the art of wood-engraving, from the number as
well as the grandeur of his works of that kind.

Chatto writes :—" There are about two hundred subjects
engraved on wood which are marked with the initials of

Albert Dürer's name; and the greater part of them, though evidently designed by the hand of a master, are engraved in a manner which certainly denotes no very great excellence. Of the remainder, which are better engraved, it would be difficult to point out one which displays execution so decidedly superior as to enable any person to say positively that it must have been cut by Albert Dürer himself. . . . Looking at the state of wood-engraving at the period when those cuts were published, I can not think that the artist who made the drawings would experience any difficulty in finding persons capable of engraving them. In most of the wood-cuts supposed to have been engraved by Albert Dürer, we find cross-hatching freely introduced : the readiest mode of producing effect to an artist drawing on wood with a pen or a black-lead pencil, but which to the wood-engraver is attended with considerable labour. Had Albert Dürer engraved his own designs, I am inclined to think that he would not have introduced cross-hatching so frequently, but would have endeavoured to attain his object by means which were easier of execution. What is termed " cross-hatching " in wood-engraving is nothing more than the black lines crossing each other, for the most part diagonally ; and in *drawing* on wood it is easier to produce a shade by this means than by thickening the lines ; but in *engraving* on wood it is precisely the reverse, for it is easier to leave a thick line than to cut out the interstices of lines crossing each other. Nothing is more common than for persons who know little of the history of wood-engraving, and still less of the practice, to refer to the frequent cross-hatching in the cuts supposed to have been engraved by Albert Dürer as a proof of their excellence ; as if the talent of the artist were chiefly displayed in such parts of the cuts as are in reality least worthy of him, and which a mere workman might execute as well." [CHATTO, pp. 233, 234.]

Dürer's earliest great work on wood, the earliest, at least, on which we have his mark, here given, was the *Apocalypse*—the Revelation of John, sixteen cuts of large folio size, "printed at Nuremberg by Albrecht Dürer, painter, in the year after the birth of Christ, 1498." Printed, he tells us, by him, the painter, with not a word of the engraver. Great in design, as are all the works of the great German artist, there is nothing here remarkable as engraving. In 1511 appeared the second of his large works on wood, the *History of the Virgin*, nineteen cuts, about 11¾ inches in height by 8¼ inches in width. It is by far the best engraving-work up to that date. The better and more elaborate drawing was already requiring a more intelligent skill in the engraver; and so the careful mechanic had become almost an artist, proving at least his capacity to see and to exactly preserve the well-drawn lines that came under his hand. Dürer's mastership in drawing had occasioned mastership in cutting, in even the mechanical execution. *Christ's Passion* (what is known as the "*Larger Passion*"), twelve cuts yet larger than those of the *History of the Virgin*, appeared about the same time ; and, a little later, he published the "*Little Passion*," a series of thirty-seven cuts. The blocks of these are in the British Museum, from an electrotype of one of which our cut facing p. 22 has been printed, the broken lines having been restored by Mr. Thurston Thompson. It fairly shows the character of Dürer's drawings, and the excellence in cutting at that time reached. These three series—the *History of the*

*Virgin*, and the two *Passions*, with Burgmair's *Procession*, to be spoken of presently—may be considered the crowning triumphs of wood-engraving at that early period.

Other cuts of Dürer's designing might be noted, of equal worth ; but his single cuts are too numerous to be even catalogued here. One, however, must not be left unmentioned—his *Arch of Maximilian*, a sort of pictorial epitome of German history, " after the manner of those erected [in stone] in honour of the Roman Emperors,"— one large composition 10 feet in height by $8\frac{1}{2}$ in width, formed of ninety-two separate pieces. Impressions of this are in the Print Room of the British Museum. The cutting is excellent.

And now we arrive at the names of early engravers, chief of whom, as " best engraver of his time " (the very supremacy proving the importance of the art), was Jerome Resch (also called André), who is said by Neudorffer, a contemporary of Dürer, to have engraved most of the Dürer designs. Dr. Conrad Peutinger, also, the Emperor Maximilian's commissioner, writes from Augsburg, in 1510, that he had brought from Nuremberg (from Dürer) the greatest part of the *Arch of Triumph*, to have the blocks engraved in Augsburg. And he gives, in his expenses of that year, the sums he had paid to Burgmair for other work as painter, and also to the wood-preparer and two engravers. And there yet exists a letter of an engraver of Antwerp, Jost Dienecker (or de Negker, so signed by himself on some of his engravings), in which he writes of the engravings for the *Wise King*, " that I am charged to prepare " (for the same Emperor Maximilian), and asks to be allowed to employ two other engravers as his assistants, in which case he will be careful to finish and

*From* Dürer's "Little Passion."

clear (or clean) them himself, "so that the engraving shall appear to be by one hand, and no one be able to know that several have worked on it."

Names also of engravers are found on the backs of blocks done for Burgmair's great work, the *Triumphs of Maximilian*, a long, stately, triumphal procession (designed and perhaps drawn on the wood by him), engraved upon 135 pieces of wood, 15 inches high, to a length of 150 feet.

We may pass by the works on wood after the drawings of Lucas Cranach and Hans Schaufflein, and those executed by Albert Altdorffer, Hans Sebald Beham, Christopher Jegher, and others. There is nothing really distinctive in the character of the *engraving*,—merely larger or smaller, all mechanical, more or less skilful, but proving how extensive was the use of wood engraving, out of which grew naturally a more accomplished mastery and greater nicety of handling. We note the perfection of this more intelligent and artful mechanism in Holbein's *Dance of Death*, published at Lyons, in 1538: forty-one cuts, engraved by Hans Lützelburger, an engraver of Basle, who is supposed to have also engraved an *Alphabet*, representing the same Death-Dance; and two other *Alphabets*, containing groups of children and peasants—all attributed to Holbein. Our reproduction, though by photographic process, and so certainly line for line and of the same size as the original, gives but an insufficient idea of the delicate beauty of Lützelburger's work. These cuts reach the high-water mark of old engraving on wood, of that method of wood-engraving which I shall have to describe as *knife work*.

Not much of this knife-cutting of the time subsequent

to Holbein need engage our attention. We have only to mention the works of John Michael Papillon (one of a

family of engravers), a French engraver of considerable merit, 1720-1768; and some cuts done in England for Croxall's *Æsop's Fables,* 1722, (possibly cut in soft metal, but still for surface-printing,) on very insufficient evidence attributed to Edward Kirkall, an excellent engraver in copper of that date. And now we reach the modern era of wood-engraving, at

*The Unjust Judge.*
From Holbein's DANCE OF DEATH.

the head of which stands the name of BEWICK.

———

THOMAS BEWICK, whose productions (as justly observed by Mr. Chatto) " recalled attention to the neglected art," was born in the neighbourhood of Newcastle-on-Tyne, in 1753. *Select Fables* (1784), drawn and engraved by him, is the first of these productions (his earlier cuts but 'prentice-work) to claim our notice. Not better engraved than the cuts in Croxall's *Fables,* we have to point to them as the deliberate beginning of a new method—*the use of white line,* instead of the old method (from the date of the

*St. Christopher* to the days of Papillon) *of always black
lines.* The cuts in Croxall's *Fables* are, indeed, of the same
character as Bewick's; such cutting of white lines for
surface-printing, readily suggested by the practice of the
copper-engraver, had, indeed, been often used before in
metal. Whether the cuts for the Croxall *Fables* were done
in metal or wood, there is no knowing. Even if in wood,
we may fairly give to Bewick the credit of adopting this
method as the principle of his work. Of it I shall have to
speak hereafter. The publication of his *General History*

From Bewick's SELECT FABLES.

*of Quadrupeds*, in 1790, established his reputation. In
1797 the *Land Birds*, in 1804 the *Water Birds*, and an
altogether new series of *Fables* in 1818, successively added
to his fame. It should be owned, and without disparage-
ment of the master, that more and more, as years went on,
he had the assistance of able pupils : Robert Johnson and
William Temple as designers, Luke Clennell, as designer
and engraver, Charlton Nesbit as engraver, William
Harvey as draughtsman and engraver. But the *Quadru-*

*peds*, the *Land* and *Water Birds* (with but few exceptions), and very many of the tail-pieces throughout his volumes are drawn and engraved by his own hands. Bewick died in 1828. Clennell's work appears largely in the tail-pieces of the *Water Birds*. He, as artist-engraver, stands beside Bewick, with a yet greater command of the graver. Nesbit, as engraver only, stands next of the Bewick school. William Harvey engraved most of the *Fables* of 1818, and had certainly equalled, if not surpassed, any of the before-named, had he not given up engraving, and confined himself to designing and drawing for engravers. His great print of the *Assassination of L. S. Dentatus*, 15 inches by $11\frac{1}{2}$, drawn and engraved by himself from Haydon's picture, though confused and otherwise faulty in style, too much in imitation of copper-plate, may yet be spoken of as the most daring and, in some respects, the most successful engraving ever attempted in wood.

Robert Branston, born at Lynn, in Norfolk, in 1778, dying in 1827, a year earlier than Bewick, shares with him the credit of raising the character of wood-engraving. Like Bewick he was brought up as a metal-engraver. His style differs from that of Bewick in being more an imitation of copper-plate, and in a consequent preference for black line as the principle and general manner of his work, though, a master of the graver, he could use white line when it pleased him. The manner of his work was also influenced by his dependence upon the drawings of Thurston, an accomplished copper-engraver, and much employed draughtsman on wood at that time. Bewick and Branston may be fairly considered as the heads of the two schools of wood-engraving, " white line " and " black line," the heads, though not the beginners of either method. John Thompson, a pupil of Branston, as *engraver only* superior to all, followed the lead of Branston.

These are the Masters of our art. Many names of good engravers besides, of that time and later, might be mentioned : William Hughes, and Hugh Hughes, Hole, Bonner, Henry White, Samuel and Thomas Williams (brothers), John Jackson, Orrin Smith, Powis, are of the principal. And some of their works will have to be referred to in the course of our instruction ; but all that seems necessary here for history is to give the salient points in the progress of engraving, to make that progress clear, and to help toward the better understanding of our manual of instruction.

# CHAPTER III.

### OF THE DIFFERENCE BETWEEN CUTTING AND ENGRAVING.

S far as I have been able to ascertain, with the one possible exception of the cuts to Croxall's *Fables,* 1722, all engravings on wood from the earliest time to the time of Bewick were done with *knives* instead of *gravers.* In France the knife-use was continued through the first quarter of the present century, until Charles Thompson (the brother of John) settled as an engraver in Paris, and took over with him the new manner. In Germany knife-work has been done, and of wonderfully fine quality, within the last few years; and may, for aught I know, be in practice still, though we are not without German artists of high talent, Kruell, of New York, and others, who only employ the graver. I can not find out when the graver (the tool always used by engravers in metal) was first used in wood, seeing nothing certain of an earlier time than Bewick. And I do not get any evidence even of the use of the *scrive,* a sort of double knife, or hollow graver, used to cut letters on timber (by. wood-carvers also) and for some years past commonly employed in America for very large work, street-posters and the like.

The *knife* instead of the *graver* was used for this simple reason; because all engravings were done upon *planks* of wood, wood cut the long way of the tree. Let anyone take a plank, a deal board, or a lengthway-cut piece of any wood, and with a " graver," a solid piece of steel, the face of the shape here given, try to cut or plough out a clean line across the grain. In any drawing there must be some lines running across. He will find that, though he may plough out a clean line, or one that shall be only not clean at the end, when running *with* the grain, *across* the grain the broken wood will fray up on each side of his furrow, rendering it impossible for him to make a clean cut. To provide against this the engraver used a knife. With the knife he made an incision against, or by the side of his drawn line—the line he had to preserve *for surface-printing*, —a mere sloping incision, which brought out no wood; he had to make a second incision to cut out a wedge-shaped piece : two cuts for one of the ploughing graver. Nor was this all ; to get this wedge of wood clear, then only outlined on two sides, he must also cut across the ends, or the wood would tear out. Four clean cuts with the knife were therefore necessary for each piece of wood to be removed, however small. Or take four cross lines, as here given. No less than thirty-two or thirty-six cuts would be required in order to leave standing clean and on the surface these four lines. It was a slow and laborious process, one that was purely mechanical, but for all work needing great exactness to be faithful to the

drawing, and for very fine work a niceness of hand which
must have been very difficult of attainment
and only to be acquired by long practice.
In some works by Papillon the subjects are
so minute (several figures, it may be, in a
cut not more than an inch in length and
half an inch in height) that it would be
almost impossible to believe they could have
been cut with knives (however thin the
knife), with at least two cuts for each piece
of wood taken out, were it not that Papillon
exactly describes the process and gives a
representation of the kind of knife used, as
here copied from him (somewhat less than
ordinary size). Well practised as he himself was, he does not make light of the difficulty of the process ; dwells, indeed, with
emphasis on the great attention and care
required in engraving kinds of lines, straight
and curved, single or crossed, the necessity
of precision in what he calls the *cut* and the
*re-cut*, dictates the manner of holding the
knife, explains that it must not be with-
drawn brusquely for fear of tearing the
grain of the wood, or of the knife being
caught in the wood-fibre when cutting across
it. Nor only does he make it clear that all
his own work, and other up to his time, was
done by means of this simple tool, of various
degrees of strength or fineness according to
the largeness or delicacy of the work ; but also he denies
the possibility of the use of the graver, even on the end of

the wood (supposing it cut in rounds, as at present is always done for graver-work). In a curious passage of his *Treatise* he states that some years previous to its publication (1766) a foreigner (" un Etranger," whom he does not condescend to name) " appeared in Paris who engraved with a graver[1] on the end of the wood, and pretended much advancement by this artifice: but this man reasoned without principles and without art ; he was ignorant of the impossibility of engraving properly on the end of the wood with such a tool, because the graver could only lift the wood, and could not cut the lines sharply and cleanly.  What is more, it renders all the lines ragged " [barbelées—bearded or tooth-edged] ; adding other good reasons proving that this method with a graver was not worth thinking of, and indeed " refuted itself."

Papillon evidently adopted his conclusions without a practical trial; and yet himself had worked with his knives on the roots of box-wood, in order to avoid the awkwardness of the grain on the plank.  Box-wood was then as now in use, but for delicate work only, and cut plank-wise. For larger work softer woods were good enough: pear and apple woods, privet, sycamore, any white wood upon which a drawing could be seen—everything being drawn line for line on the plank ; the engraver's business simply to cut away the white spaces between the lines, cutting, as before said, with knives in the smaller spaces, and with chisels and gouges clearing away the larger to a sufficient depth to escape the ink in printing.  Bearing in mind the four incisions for getting out the smallest piece of wood with a knife, the reader will at once perceive the great gain over

---

[1] Might this foreigner be the English engraver of the cuts to Croxall's Fables ?

knife-work obtained by the modern engraver, who uses
*the graver on the end of the wood,* in Papillon's "impossible"
manner.

It has been said that all knife-work is purely mechanical.   It is strictly so if between *mechanism* and *art* we
insist upon an absolute distinction.   But even so we must
still allow a most artistic perception in the best knife-user,
and confess the delicacy of nice manual skill in the best of
that old knife-work, in the cuts from Dürer's drawings,
and in the exquisite knife-renderings after Holbein.   Also,
when the draughtsman on wood was also the engraver, he
needed not to draw every line for exact following.   He
might alter the bearing of a line, or its form, or strength ;
or he might cut a series of shading lines, without having
them first drawn.   But this would be quite an exception
to the ordinary practice ; and, indeed, Papillon claims that
he was the first who, as he made his own drawings, trusted
as he went on to his judgment in fitting lines for his
shadows and tinted parts.   This would be, indeed, a beginning of intelligent art.   But the general practice was
only more or less skilful mechanism.

With the use of the graver began what we may more
properly call the *art* of wood-engraving.   The engraver
was still to be an engraver of work to be printed from the
surface, from a block on which the picture stood in relief.
But the graver could now be used, not merely to cut away
the wood.   It could be also used, as in copper-engraving,
*to cut a line with meaning,* a line which, though in the
print it would appear white, would be none the less
expressive.   Supposing the subject to be entirely engraved
in this manner (see Bewick's cut at page 25, and Clennell's
at page 34), the *effect* would be simply the reverse of

L. Clennel, Sc.

copper-plate, all the drawing rendered in white lines instead of black. But as in even these two cuts there is,
and in almost all subjects must be, an amount of open
space, white with but few lines upon it, those lines would
be cut, or left in relief, in the old manner. The combination of the two methods will be yet more observable in
Branston's work, in our frontispiece.

Let the student now carefully examine and compare the
several engravings we have given after Dürer and Holbein,
and by Williams, Branston, and Clennell. The Dürer,
however well cut, cannot be considered as anything more
than mechanical. Lützelburger's work on the *Dance of
Death*, though mechanical also, is the mechanism of an
artist, a man who perceived and felt the value of every
line he cut or, rather, which he left standing. If this is
not exactly art, it is something closely akin to it. Williams's work hardly equals this, although it, too, is good
work, done by an artist, and done with all the advantage
of the graver. Here, as in the Dürer and Holbein designs,
the designer, George Cruikshank, drew every line. To
make my distinction more clear, I would call these *wood-
cuts* excellent certainly, but with less of *art* in them than
in the *wood-engravings* by Branston and Clennell, to be now
compared with them. In the Branston engraving, though
much would be drawn by Thurston in lines, some would
be a mere wash of colour, for which the engraver would
have to find lines. Not mere literal fidelity in following
the lines drawn, as in the Dürer cut, nor only the most
artistic appreciation of their value, as in the cuts by Lützelburger and Williams; but, in this Branston engraving,
something more has been required—intelligence in rendering the intention of the drawing, while having to express

D

much of it after his own fashion, associated with appreciative fidelity to lines meaned to be exactly followed. In the engraving by Clennell, all the lines are Clennell's : probably not a line drawn with the pencil, but every line drawn by his graver. This is what I would call art. This constitutes the difference, or distinction, I would like to establish between wood-cuts and wood-engravings, between mechanism and art. Any lad with good sight and fair and continual practice can become sooner or later an expert mechanic, a close and tolerably satisfactory clearer or carver-out of the spaces between lines drawn on a block, be they never so small, whether with a knife or with a graver. He may do this to the wonder and admiration of the untaught and unknowing critic, who, finding an almost incomprehensible fineness or, I would say, closeness together of lines, exclaims, "What a beautiful engraving!" when from first to last it may only afford proof of good sight, much patience, and the exactness of an accomplished mechanic : only that, at the same time utterly devoid of beauty as an engraving:—indeed, save to excuse the critic's lack of discrimination, hardly worthy of the name of *an engraving.* Let us keep that name for works of art only, and so mark the distinction between *wood-cuts* and *wood-engravings !*

Yet fine work—that is, minute work—is not to be despised. Nor let it be thought that even in close preserving of fac-simile lines an artist will not have the advantage. " The eye sees what it brings the means of seeing ;" and the artist's eye is the more educated. The artist, if master of the special tools required, will always be distinguished in his work. Not less than artistic perception was wanted for Williams's excellent keeping of Cruikshank's drawing.

We have but one Lützelburger among the wood-cutters of
old time; and it would be no undue honour to him to
think of him as an artist. The cuts or engravings I have
chosen for examples of work were not meant to mark in-
vidiously the status of the cutters or engravers, but to
contrast the two styles, to emphasize a distinction necessary to be borne in mind in the teaching I have in view :
the distinction and real difference between *cutting* and
*engraving*, however the two may be combined, or whatever
the difficulty of classification.

To repeat, for the sake of being thoroughly understood.
The mere cutting away of wood, so as to leave intact certain lines drawn clearly on the surface of the block (such
drawings as those, for instance, by Tenniel in his cartoons
for *Punch*) can hardly be called an art; albeit, if the cutter
be an artist, his character will generally be more or less
manifest,—that is to say, his work will stand out from
among the mass of fac-simile-cutting as having in it something of taste or beauty, perhaps even of subtle truth to
the original, which has escaped the most perfect of un-
artistic mechanics. He must, indeed, in that particular
work be also a perfect mechanic. Else there is no fair
comparison between the two productions. We can not
*compare* what is only artistic, and not of mechanical excellence, with what is only excellent mechanism. Each will
be good of its kind, but there can be no comparison.

In thus defining *cutting* and *engraving*, let me say again,
I am only endeavouring to show the difference between
*the mechanical* and *art*. It is a vital point.

"Black line," which is called fac-simile (supposed to be
the identical lines of the drawing preserved in the cutting),
is mechanical work, though it may be better done by an

artist than by the mechanic. "White line," which is drawing with the graver (the counterpart of the black line of the copper-plate engraver or etcher)—"white line" alone is art.

# CHAPTER IV.

## OF THE TOOLS REQUIRED FOR ENGRAVING ON WOOD.

HESE tools are required for an engraver's outfit: an assortment of *gravers*, an *oil-stone*, a *sand-bag* or cushion, an *eye-glass*, a *lamp*, and a *globe*. The outfit is not very expensive; twenty-five shillings will cover the whole cost, at something under the following prices :—

|                                      | £ | s. | d. |
|--------------------------------------|---|----|----|
| Gravers, twelve (with handles), each |   |    |    |
| 6d. . . . . . . | 0 | 6 | 0 |
| An oil-stone . . . . . | 0 | 2 | 0 |
| A sand-bag . . . . . | 0 | 1 | 0 |
| An eye-glass . . . . . | 0 | 1 | 0 |
| A lamp . . . . . . | 0 | 10 | 0 |
| A globe . . . . . | 0 | 5 | 0 |
|                                      | £1 | 5 | 0 |

The GRAVERS (one of which is here represented, reduced to about three-fourths of its size, to suit the width of our page) can be had of almost any good cutler, ready set in their handles ; or the gravers may be bought of the cutler, and the handles, to any preferred pattern, of a turner. In

America a bit of cork often serves for handle. Our English handles are of wood, of various shapes and lengths, with brass ferules at the end to prevent splitting. The most convenient shape I have found to be that in the cut. It is of course round when first had from the turner. The under-side must be cut off, that the graver may not roll about on the table. Several gravers will be required, as they are of different sizes and shapes, as shown in the cut below. A dozen may be quite sufficient.

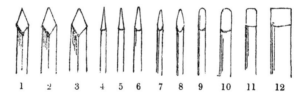

All these I have called *gravers*, since they are all tools used in engraving : but the name is generally confined to the first three, which are tools similar to the gravers used by copper-engravers, only they are not so square, but more lozenge or diamond-shaped, as in 1, 2, 3.

*Tint-tools*, or *shade-tools*, is the name by which 4, 5, 6, 7,

8, are known, since they are used for cutting tints or
shades in which the series of lines are intended to be
exactly or nearly parallel, or equidistant. It will be
noticed that 7 and 8 are slightly rounded in the sides,
owing to which a varying line can be more easily cut by
them than by the flat-sided tools, 4, 5, 6. The tools 9 and
10 are solid gouges used only for clearing out small pieces
in spaces between the lines : made solid because the ordinary hollow gouge would be too easily broken in the
hard box-wood ; and 11 and 12 are flat chisels for clearing down the outer edges, to avoid the ink in printing.

The three gravers proper, 1, 2, 3, are of different sizes
for degrees of finer or larger work ; and the whole of an
engraving, including tints, may be done with these by a
sure hand. It is only a greater regularity that is to be
obtained by use of the tint-tool. I have been in the
habit of using the graver instead of the tint-tool whenever
I cared more for freedom than uniformity of line. A very
slightly rounded tool, 7, 8, allowing of some limited variety
of line, yet not tending to so much divergence as the graver,
was always a favourite tool with me for soft and delicate
and nicely graded shades. Of course it may be had of
any degree of strength or fineness, according to the line
to be cut.

The three gravers and five tint-tools seem to me to be
enough for all kinds of work ; but I have known engravers
to use twenty or more. Powis would take up a different
tint-tool for every variation of colour in his skies and
other shades. I think this, however, quite unnecessary.
The wedge-like shape of gravers and tint-tools shows at
once that leaning a little more or less heavily will make a
deeper or shallower, a wider or narrower, cut or incision ;

and the accomplished engraver will trust rather to his hand than merely to the size of the tool. It must be noted that the graver and tint-tool when purchased is always sharp on the underside, as at 1; therefore, to cut a wider line without going to an unnecessary and mischievous depth, it is requisite that the under part of the graver or tint-tool should be rubbed down on the oil-stone and rounded, less or more, according to the desired increase of size. No. 1 will be kept perfectly fine, for the finest work; 2 very slightly rounded, its square shape helping also to cut a broader line; 3 rounded, as in the diagram given of shapes and sizes, for yet larger work; 4, 5, 6, 7, 8, varying also as there shown. I have no intention of limiting the number of tools. I have never more than this number in use; but if anyone would like a larger number and greater variety, the only objection is the possibility of too great a dependence on the graver, and consequently less trust in the hand. On such a point everyone must judge for himself.

Let it be noted, also, that the tools when bought will often be found to be too hard and brittle, so that the points easily break off. They then need *tempering*, a very easy process. A poker or other bar or piece of iron made red-hot, the graver is laid against it, from near the graver-point to about three-quarters of an inch of the graver's length, and turned repeatedly till it becomes of a pale gold colour, when it should be quickly dropped into oil, and left in the oil to cool. If kept too long on the hot iron, it will turn blue, and become too soft.

The tools are also generally a little too long for use. This depends entirely on the engraver's hand; some engravers like a longer tool than can be used by others. A piece broken off from the butt, or a shorter handle, may accommodate this. When from wear a tool becomes too short, a longer handle is available. It is well to let the cutler grind off a portion of the backs of the tools (as from *a* to *b* in cut of graver, at p. 38). This will save your time when you come to sharpen them on the oil-stone.

The general use of the CHISEL and the GOUGE requires no explanation. I find the smaller chisel most serviceable if slightly rounded at the angles. See 11.

In choosing your tools, be careful to see that they are perfectly straight! There can be no command over a crooked one.

The SCRIVE, a tool already spoken of, is shaped like two knives, or as a hollow graver. It is of no use on the end of the wood, but is well employed in engraving large subjects on the plank,—the double cutting making a clean furrow even across the grain.

The OIL-STONE required should be a piece of rather soft "Turkey stone," of good greyish colour. A hard stone will necessitate too much labour in sharpening the tools. One too soft, and too freely wearing down the steel, will create a burr, a rough turned edge or point, by no means desirable. What would be good for a penknife or a razor will serve equally well for the graver. For size, say a piece about six to eight inches long, by two wide, which may be set in a piece of wood, with or without a lid; or a piece of flat stone, that will lie steady, may be used unset.

The SAND-BAG is a leather cushion filled with sand (its shape sufficiently shown at p. 55), on which to rest the block, so that it may be readily turned while held firmly in the hand. The engraver may choose what size he thinks most convenient: from four to six inches across may give him choice. If the sand-bag be too hard, a little beating, careful not to burst it, will soften it enough for pleasant use.

An EYE-GLASS, such as watch-makers use for magnifying, seems to be considered a necessity for engravers, though I have never used one, perhaps from being both short-sighted and strong-sighted. It will certainly be wanted for the distressingly minute work now in fashion. It may be held on the eye, or fixed in a frame, as shown in the cut at the end of the book ; there will be more freedom in the first way. Let the engraver, however, trust his own unaided sight as far as he can ! Once in the habit of using the glass, he will not be able to give it up, and let him, if possible, not confine the use to one eye ! I have known the sight of an eye lost: not the eye using the glass, but the eye that was habitually unemployed. That is to say, the sight of the unused eye was lost for engraving-work. If a magnifier must be used, I believe it would be much better to use spectacles instead of the single eye-glass. At all events it would be worth while to try spectacles first.

The LAMP, for work at night, may be of such construction as most pleases, or best suits the engraver. He can use oil or gas : but, it need hardly be said, that the steadier the light, the more pleasant it will be for him and the better for his eyes. Nothing will hurt them more than a flickering light.

A GLOBE is required because the ordinary light of an

oil-lamp or single gas-jet is not strong enough for an engraver's work. The light must be from a single burner, in order to avoid the confusion that would arise from cross-shadows. To concentrate and intensify the light of this single burner, either of two things may be used : a hollow glass globe of some six, seven, or eight inches in diameter, filled with water (see cut at p. 45), or what is called a "bull's eye," a piece of solid glass round on one side, and flat on the other, as if it had been cut off a solid globe. The globe or bull's eye is placed between the lamp and the block. If the bull's eye is used it needs to be mounted in a frame, or on some sort of stand. The globe can be had at any glass house, with a solid glass stem and foot, to stand of itself. There will be two advantages in the use of the globe. Taking up more room than the bull's eye, and also from being filled with water, it keeps off the heat of the flame from the head of the engraver, and also the water can be coloured blue, and so softened for the engraver's eyes. To colour the water you have only to lay a halfpenny, or any piece of copper, for a few minutes in a saucer and cover it with nitrous or nitric acid. A very slight corrosion of the copper will give enough colouring matter for the water in the globe. Let this be as pure as can be had. The acid will keep the water clear for months.

These are all the tools needed to set up an engraver on wood. A place of habitation or work-room, the more comfortable the better, a good north light so as not to be troubled with sunshine, a table or bench, and a chair or stool (better without a cushion), may also be of advantage. But these are not tools.

"May be of advantage," is said, for there is no know-

ing what will happen in coming days through " new de-
partures and developments." It has been gravely inti-
mated of late (and in quarters where engraving is
extensively employed, and where some consequent knowledge should be expected) that all these things, workroom,
bench, and stool, may be advantageously dispensed with;
that with block in one hand and graver in the other, the
engraver will walk into the full glare of sunlight and,
with abundant nerve-power and condensation of will,
engrave directly what he sees before him, forest scenery,
wind-driven clouds, grouped figures, or what not; and
engraving "from nature" will supersede the now too
much imitated photography. How can we dare to laugh?
Did not Papillon prove the impossibility of engraving
with a graver on the end of the wood? Yet I would
not advise the expenditure of much time in this new
direction.

And so long as sunlight dazzles and disturbs the engraver, who, though he requires a shadow thrown from
his line, that he may know what he has cut, yet likes not
excess of illumination, it may be well, instead of stepping
from his window into the air, that he put up a "blind,"
both to moderate the light and to keep cool his eyes and
head. A light frame with tissue, or "silver," paper
strained across it will answer the purpose. He may also
at all times shield his eyes by wearing a light shade at his
work. It can be made of black silk or calico over thin
card-board. Black is better than green. Or if no friendly
woman's hand will make this for him, let him make shift
with a piece of stiff brown paper, cut into shape and held
on his head by a string.

The friendly woman reminds me of the invariable use of

*he* and *him.* Let it be said then that wherever in the instructions here given the terms *he* and *him* are used, *she* and *her* may be understood as equally intended. No artist work can be more suitable for women than our art of wood-engraving, in which already several, Mary Byfield and Eliza Thompson, and others, have distinguished themselves.

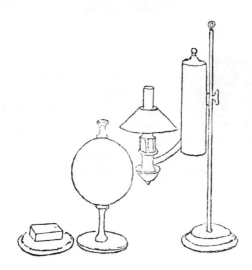

GLOBE AND LAMP.

## CHAPTER V.

### OF DRAWING ON WOOD FOR ENGRAVING.

N engraver of any ability may engrave upon a plain block, a block on which there is no drawing, no indication whatever of what he is about to do. He can engrave (as he can draw) "out of his own head," improvising his subject; or he may engrave from a picture or copy before him, as is done by the engraver in steel or copper. But he has not the facilities of the copper-engraver, who can draw or trace his most delicate outlines, strengthen, alter, or remove them as needful, and then add the shadows, elaborating more and more as he may find occasion. The wood-engraver can not so alter or remove. Everything is done at once, and what is cut remains. He may indeed cut away more wood, so lightening and sometimes giving tone to certain parts of his subject; he may clear away altogether : but there is the limit of his power of alteration or amendment. It is therefore desirable that there should be some guide for him on the block before he begins to engrave. In all "black-line" work, such as has been already described, it is absolutely necessary to

have every line drawn upon the wood, except perhaps a
mere series of shadow lines, which the engraver might be
allowed to give at his own discretion, but even then the
colour to be obtained by those lines would have to be
shown by a tint washed on the block. The fineness or
coarseness of these shadow lines, perhaps their direction
and character, might be left to the engraver. Not so much
as this was left to the early wood-cutters or engravers.
Every line was distinctly drawn. The engraver saw all
before him. He had only mechanically and servilely to
cut away the parts left white. Later Papillon, as he tells
us, trusted to his own taste in shadows and, drawing for
himself, did not draw line for line where only a regular
series of lines or a tint was wanted. Bewick in his
earliest work, engraving after the manner of copper, may
have engraved upon a black block (blackened that he
might better see the lines he cut), without drawing of any
kind, improvising as he went on : his work was " white
line," he was always drawing with his graver. The only
advantage of this method of improvisation was as an
exercise for himself, toward obtaining a more confident
and masterful handling. He perhaps learned his preference for " white line " from this practice on the surface-
blackened block. For his later more careful and elaborate
work he did not scorn the advantage of a drawing on the
wood before he began to engrave. During my own time,
from 1828 (the year of Bewick's death), there has been no
engraving except with a drawing first made. None in
England, I should say, for Anderson and Adams, and
other early American engravers, beginning with copies
from English work, engraved on the blackened block, with
only their originals before them. These they copied, line

for line, and marvellously well : not, however, refusing the
aid of the first drawing, but ignorant of its use, having no
instruction in that method of procedure.  For practice, in
order to get command of the graver, and to learn to draw
with it, this black-block work can not be over-valued ; but
nevertheless the drawing on the block is of advantage.
Nor only an advantage : in all cases that, in some it is an
absolute necessity,—owing to what has been already stated,
the difficulty, one might almost say the impossibility, of
alterations of a wood-engraving.

It may then be taken as established in the order of
procedure toward producing a wood-engraving that there
is in the first instance some sort of drawing on the block.
How this shall be made is our next inquiry.

In the first place the wood is cut in rounds from the log,
planed to an even thickness to the height of type (about
seven-eighths of an inch), in order that the engravings and
types may be set up together ; it is then scraped to a perfectly smooth and polished surface.  Then, partly to get
rid of the yellow colour of the wood and the differences of
grain, but chiefly because a pencil can scarcely make a
mark upon the polished surface, a "ground" is laid upon
it.  A little dust from a "Bath brick," a kind of soft
brick, used for cleaning knives, which crumbles easily, and
is not gritty, may be rubbed over it.  This gives a certain
very slight roughness, so that a pencil can freely work on
the wood.  One objection to this ground is that it is likely
to be too rough, and so prevent a sharp thin line, most
desirable in a drawing in lines only.  Another objection is
that some remaining grit may break the point of the
graver.  A better ground, therefore, I think, is Chinese
or permanent white (water-colour, of course) laid on the

wood with a full brush, and then smoothed over and wiped with the ball of the thumb, until the least possible quantity remains, just enough to partly hide the wood grain, and to give a texture to hold the pencil. There are draughts-men who, sometimes ignorantly, and sometimes because a rough ground enables them more quickly to scramble over their drawing, will plaster a thick coat of white over the block. To the great hindrance of the engraver. I have known this coat of paint to be so thick that it had to be washed off before a proof could be printed from the block, after which washing it was found that the graver had been cutting only in a coat of paint, scarcely at all in the wood, and that the unfortunate workman had thrown away his labour, and also lost the drawing. I am giving an extreme and an infrequent case; but the too great thickness of ground is not infrequent, and can not be too strongly condemned. Even when there is not this most objectionable thickness to so harmful an extent, there may be sufficient body, especially if there is gum or spirit in the white, to cause it to peel off, the graver lifting flakes, to the loss of drawing. In fact, the thinner the ground the better it is for the engraver: it can not be too thin. The conscientiously careful draughtsman will find his ad-vantage, also, in the purity and firmness of his line, and the assurance that his drawing will not be rubbed off before the engraver is through with his work. Drawn loosely on a rough ground, the engraver can hardly help losing much of the drawing—the more delicate lines, cer-tainly—before he can complete his task. Drawn firmly (which is only possible on a ground not rough), the last lines to be engraved should, with a little care, remain as sharp and clear as they were at first. Surely this should

E

be of importance to the draughtsman as well as the engraver; and though the engraver make his own drawing, it were not well to have the trouble of re-drawing, occasioned by the rubbing-out of parts from a rough ground.

So far we have been considering only drawings in pencil to be engraved in fac-simile, where the loss of lines may be of most importance. But even where the draughtsman contents himself in certain parts of his subject—skies or masses of tint of any kind—with expressing only colour, by rubbing in the same with no distinct lines, it may be well to draw firmly. On the true rendering of colour, the exact gradations between light and dark, the artist depends for his effect; and how be sure of that, if the drawing be fugitive? In pen-and-ink drawings also (here speaking for the draughtsman's benefit) the thinnest possible ground will be best. A thick ground will be apt to be taken up by the pen, and mix muddyingly with the ink. This most thin ground, again, will be best suited to drawings partly or wholly in wash.

What is called a " washed drawing " is one in which shadows, broad tints, such as sky, ground, walls, (indeed all masses of colour,) are washed in broadly with a brush in sepia or India ink, and only the details given or merely emphasized with pencil. This process of washing is precisely the same on wood as on paper; there is no need to describe it. In such a drawing it is left to the engraver to invent the lines which shall best reproduce the varieties of colour or shade, or best represent the forms and textures of substance given in the drawing. It was in this manner of " wash " that our best painters in water-colour —W. L. Leitch, Duncan, Dodgson, and others—made their drawings upon wood: usually landscapes, for which the manner is more suitable than fac-simile. In figure-subjects also, especially of a large size, the same wash-method obtains to a great extent. It is not always either convenient or of any advantage to draw a subject through-out in lines; and few painters are capable of doing it. It is peculiarly the business of the engraver to invent the lines by which form, substance, and texture can best be represented. But a treatise on drawing is not to be given here. All that seems to be required here is the pointing out what is of importance in relation to the engraver. Well for him if he be associated with an artist able to understand the necessity of good and careful drawing, and other conditions of the engraver's work. Better still for him if he be capable of sometimes making his own draw-ings, and so being occasionally independent of outside slovenliness or ignorance.

And not only for such independence: for no man will be completely furnished as an engraver without some power of drawing. Though he may not have the painter's faculty, he must have knowledge of form and effect, or he cannot do justice to drawings with form and effect given to him to engrave. Only to preserve lines laid down to guide him is the province of a mechanic; nor will any mere servile keeping of form or colour by unmeaning lines, entitle the engraver to the name of artist.

## CHAPTER VI.

OF THE METHOD OF PROCEDURE IN ENGRAVING.

OW the engraver shall set about his work; what method to pursue from first to last; nay, first how to fit himself to become an engraver. A child may begin with carving his name, or by attempting to cut any few lines drawn for him on the block of wood. But a Manual is not intended for a child: rather is it for one too old or without opportunity to be under the supervision and con‐tinual instruction given to an apprentice. And to such an one, young man or woman, boy or girl, I would most dis‐tinctly and emphatically say: DO NOT BEGIN WITH ME‐CHANISM! Begin with a desire for art—to be an artist! Let no would-be engraver be content to become a me‐chanic! The days of mere mechanism in wood-cutting are numbered. Some one of the many processes for the reproduction of fac-simile drawing will assuredly take the place of the work of the wood-cutter. Already, I think, fac-simile work is done better, and at less cost, without the intervention of the "engraver." It is only the art, the artistic part of engraving, that is still worth our attention.

That artistic part is drawing with the graver. Learn, then, first to draw: to see form, and, after earnest endeavour, to be able to express it in the easiest way, by charcoal or chalk or pencil upon paper. It is much easier to learn to draw in this way than to learn to draw with the graver. When you can draw—I do not say design— but when you can only draw with some facility of hand, and some knowledge of what you are drawing, then, and not till then, give your attention to engraving!

The mere order of procedure we may now set forth with such minuteness of detail as seems necessary.

Jackson in his " Practice of Wood-Engraving " [*Treatise* by Chatto and Jackson], carefully describes the different qualities of wood, so that the engraver may know how to choose it for himself. Papillon informs us even of the right posture in which to sit, for the comfort of the sitter, and for his stomach's sake as well as for convenience in his work. There is no longer need for Jackson's description of the kinds of wood, as the preparation of boxwood for engravers has become, since his time, so regular and extensive a business that no engraver now has to cut up his own logs, or even to square the rounds of wood sawn out of the same. He can always buy his blocks of any size, at from a penny to twopence the square inch (with an extra charge for joining pieces together, which is necessary in all large work), and he may depend upon the preparer for quality. All that need here be said as regards the wood is that white specks (because the white is too soft to stand) and red rings (which are apt to sink) have to be rejected. A clear yellow colour denotes the best quality of wood, the evener the colour, of course, the better for the drawing, though mere discolouration may not be

any detriment to the engraving. Papillon's elaborate pre-
parations for comfortable sitting may be passed by with
the remark that lounging will not be the attitude of an
earnest worker. Let it be taken for granted, then, that
our engraver is provided with a bench or table firmly set,
in a good light, and of a height convenient for himself;
that he has a chair or stool to sit on (or he may stand,
though hardly with the same convenience); that he has
his gravers, sand-bag, oil-stone, eye-glass (or spectacles),
at his hand; and his block, with some sort of drawing
upon it; his lamp and globe (or bull's eye) also ready
against the hours of darkness.

His first business is to sharpen his gravers, supposing
that he has them already rubbed down to their several
sizes. Much of the pleasantness of his work—one might
say the ease thereof—will depend on this. Good work is
not done with blunt tools, and it is well to have them not
only sharp, but in good shape, fairly adapted to the purpose of their use. Something might be said, too, of
exactness in any one thing, even in what may seem so
small a thing as tool-sharpening, helping toward a
general habit of exactness, to advantage in things of
more importance. The tool should be held firmly, so as
to present its face to the stone at the angle shown in the
figure of a graver at p. 38, which is the best angle for
cutting. The angle more obtuse, the graver will not cut
so well; the angle more acute, it will be unpleasantly
weak. Keep the face perfectly flat and square with the
sides, not one-sided; and rub it up and down the stone,
well supplied with oil, not confined to exactly the same
track, which would wear the stone into ruts. Work it
steadily, so as to keep the face always even; and, if it be

not easy to hold it firmly and move forcibly enough with one hand, press on the belly of the tool with the second finger of the other hand. Observe that the tool should work along the stone side-ways, to-and-fro, as on the dotted lines here shown. The face made, *to the very point*, pass the sides, also perfectly flat and evenly on the stone, to take off any burr on the edges of the face ; and very gently draw the belly or under part of the tool over the stone, to take off the burr, and also to preserve the size. The shape of the rounded shade-tools (see 7, 8, p. 38) must also be carefully preserved. Your finest graver will not be touched on the belly : you want it as fine as possible.

Your gravers sharpened, you want to know how to hold them. Lay the tool in the hollow of your hand, the back against the hand as you would hold a dinner-knife, but rather closer to the ball of the thumb, against which the tool-handle will rest. Then turn your hand over, as of course you cut with the belly of the tool downwards. The figure below, better than any words, will teach you farther.

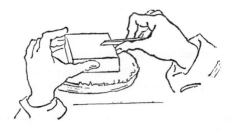

The cutting is, of course, made from right to left. The thumb pressing against the block is to prevent the possibility of slipping.  When the block is larger, it may press against the fore-finger of the left-hand, placed to meet it on the block, or merely rest upon the face of the block, still acting as a stay to the graver-blade, which moves to-and-fro beside it, guided by the right fore-finger.  The graver cuts like a plough, and always from right to left, unless you are left-handed.

Your drawing on the block is in pencil, drawn in very faintly or loosely, and you are afraid almost of breathing on it (the day being damp), afraid, whatever the weather, that your hand going over it may rub it out.  It is well to be careful of a slight pencil-drawing.  I think there is no need of the " chin-shade " invented by Papillon, and recommended by Jackson ; but it may be well to cover your drawing, as you can only work on a small portion at a time.  Take, therefore, a bit of bees-wax, and rub enough on the sides of the block just to make them sticky ; then stretch a piece of thin smooth paper flat on the face of the block, and fasten the same with the pressure of your thumb-nail to the sides.  It will not be so fast as to prevent your lifting it frequently so as to see more than the small piece of your drawing where you have torn off the paper for your working.  Do look frequently, to keep a knowledge of the whole in mind !  As you proceed to undertake large works, this frequent reference is most important.

Now begin to engrave your drawing, matters little what ; perhaps a copy of one of Bewick's earlier cuts, or something your own fancy may have suggested to you, drawn in wash, or with no more pencil than has helped to define forms.  Try how you can imitate the Bewick cut, or produce in intelligible lines of similar character your own design.  Or if you do not see your way to this (though I

would rather you began with a drawing, copied from a
fairly bold engraving), wash a dark tint over your block
(that you may see the lines you cut), and try what sort of
a drawing you can make with your graver only. At first
you may take only a single graver (size 2 or 3), and merely
cut a few *not unmeaning* lines—something which has form
in it—in order to learn not only how the graver cuts, but
how to cut with it to definite purpose, making it obedient
to your hand, whether for depth or direction of line. Practise well this " white-line " work, this drawing with the
graver ! You may vary your practice, if it so please you,
by endeavouring to cut a few lines in relief, clearing away
the rest of the wood, and leaving them standing undamaged
on the surface ; but this (it cannot be said too often) is
merely mechanical, easy enough of performance without
long course of trial. The first thing to conquer is the
command of your graver in cutting lines as surely as you
would draw them with a pencil. Bear in mind that
engraving is only drawing with a graver ; the mere
mechanism of leaving lines drawn for you, or by you, with
pen or pencil, any unintelligent but careful handicrafts-
man can accomplish. That last is but a question of steady
hand, good eye-sight, and patient attention ; it needs the
brain and taste of an artist to do the other.

In copying from any engraving, with or without drawing, in order to get command of the graver and to obtain
some knowledge of the different purposes and values of
certain kinds of line, you must recollect that what appears
in the print before you is just the reverse of what it was
in the engraving. You have then to reverse your drawing or engraving, and it is wrong teaching (Ruskin notwithstanding) to tell you that you will learn free-handed-

ness, either in drawing or engraving, by *direct copy* of an engraving. How is it possible to copy directly unless you draw or engrave with your left hand ? The engraver has to see everything reversed.

In advising the student (would-be artist) to begin with "white line," I am aware that I depart from the usual custom, which has been to begin with "black line" mechanism. I do not see how any perfection in mechanism leads up to art; and it is the making.of artist-engravers that I have in view. I differ also from Jackson's recommendation (" Practice of Engraving," *Treatise*, p. 501) of the cutting of parallel lines to produce a tint, as the first practice for an engraver, in order that he may obtain a steady hand. I differ from him entirely, believing that an even tint is by no means an easy thing for a beginner, by no means of the first importance, and also that any other practice will give him steadiness of hand just as well. Not mere steadiness of hand, but to cut a line, regular or irregular, *at your will*, is the thing to be mastered. And be sure that there is *will* and *intention*, and *a reason for your so cutting it !* Do not be content if you have, I would say, never so small a piece, of "only colour" even, to represent, to represent it with *any* unconsidered lines ! Surely that smallest piece of "only colour" means something. Is it sky, or stone, rough substance or smooth ?˙ Is it hair or water, a flat surface or round ? Recollect always that you are drawing with your graver, and unmeaning lines of either graver or pencil are not drawing. In a painting such scumbling may pass ;—colour is of itself expressive ; it may be sufficient in wash or pencil in the drawing for the engraver. But in the engraving everything is represented by lines,

and inexpressive lines are not good engraving. A habit
of always considering fitness of line—not only thinking
how close together or wide apart your lines shall be, nor
even content with giving a right direction to them,—the
habit of considering, also, what line will be the most expressive for that particular purpose, will help you in time
to an impromptu correctness of line, and stamp your work
as artistic. The careless system of "any lines will do,"
especially if so fine that they may not be noticed, prevails
too much; but the finest work should be as well considered as the coarsest (it were better to say the minutest
as the largest or boldest), or the production will have no
claim to be what an artist means by *fine* work. Again and
again it has to be insisted on that every line should have
its meaning, the justifying reason for its use. Does this
seem "too hard," too much to be required of the young
engraver? There is nothing like beginning well. Well-
begun is half-done. Starting well equipped and in the
right direction, is good beginning of a journey. Why
waste time upon the characterless work which will not
help you to become an engraver; but which may, through
the easy force of careless habit, prevent your returning
upon a better way, even when you find out your mistake?

As your graver begins to act at your bidding, so that
you use it readily as a pencil, practise what you will,
choosing your examples (as time and opportunity permit)
from the best masters, to a selection of whose works you
will be referred further on. If you have not these guides
before you, the more necessary it will be for you to think
of the lines proper for your subject, as you will then have
to invent them. Here, in these pages, is something to set
you on your way. You may learn from engravings here

given what kind of line will suit a sky, what a face, what
a piece of rock or ground.  Such methods of line may be
called conventional : nevertheless, they have been first
adopted by masters as expressive and characteristic, and
are valuable so far, however much a mere formal adherence
to them might lead you to become only mannered and
monotonous.  Do not despise these attempts, even if they
be no more than indications ; but, while honouring them,
think for yourself !   There may be new and better
methods, not always to be found through simply disregard-
ing and despising the old.

Tints you will not find so difficult as Mr. Jackson
seemed to think.   Here, do not confine yourself to two or
three forms of line because they happen to come most
easily to you ; but, always following out the processes of
thought before recommended, and in all things necessary,
let the form and direction of your lines be as suitable as
you can make them to your subject.  Some engravers,
and of no mean ability, having found that they can cut
certain tints more easily or better than other tints, limit
their variety to these.  It is not well that an artist should
be so narrowed, so marked by manner.

If you engrave from your own drawings, you will re-
joice in your freedom from interference.  If you have, as
probably will be the case, to be most generally employed
upon the drawings of other men, you must, of course,
more or less accommodate yourself to their views, even
sometimes although their instructions may but hamper
you.   The painter may not in every case understand that
an engraving is a translation into another language ; he
may be in the position of an Italian, who knowing only his
own language cannot fairly judge of a translation from

Italian into English. The mere draughtsman on the wood may trouble you with offensive or only useless lines, sometimes with fac-simile over a wash of colour, which it may be impossible or undesirable to engrave ; or he may give you white paint upon the white wood, and you can not give degrees of white, every white being absolutely white in an engraving. In such cases you must steer according to circumstances, as you best can, between your own knowledge and the ignorant requisitions of your employers, artists or others ; but while you carefully study the style and endeavour to faithfully render the manner of your draughtsman, do not submit to any abandonment of the principles of intelligent engraving, not even for the sake of praise from an unintelligent critic. Never let your engraving be a lie ! Be honest even in engraving in wood ! Strictly obey the one law—*Every line should be drawn by the graver !*

Of PROOF-TAKING something has to be said. Proof impressions, when they cannot be obtained from a printer (and it is not every printer who is capable of printing wood-engravings), must be taken by the engraver himself. Sometimes it is not worth while to employ a printer, perhaps, for a very small block ; sometimes the engraver is uncertain of his work and would see a proof before he can decide that it is finished. Let him therefore furnish himself, in addition to the tools for engraving, with

> Some India-paper,
> Printers' ink,
> An ink-ball,
> A burnisher or a paper-knife.

The INDIA-PAPER may be had of the wood-preparer, at from sixpence to a shilling for a large sheet, nearly four feet by three. It is only this paper which will serve for proofs : its texture being soft, and, from having no size in it, of the nature of blotting paper. The impression will be taken on the smoother side, after first carefully scraping from both sides any pieces of flint or straw or other matter, which else might bruise the face of the block.

PRINTERS' INK " for proving," of the very best (ten shillings the pound) can be bought of any printers' ink maker, in small tins, or jars containing a quarter of a pound, which kept covered and out of all dust, will last a long time.

The INK-BALL may be home-made ; wool covered with unribbed silk or kid leather (the sleeves of old-fashioned long white gloves were most fit for the purpose). The ball is to be stuffed so tightly as to give a good spring in it ; and may have sufficient handle in a knot of the covering where it is drawn together ; or the more fastidious engraver may prefer to have a handle expressly turned for it, with a socket into which to place the wool. The size may be at the user's convenience : a couple of inches across, or larger. A " composition " ball may also be procured of the manufacturers of printers' rollers. The silk or leathern ball has answered with me.

The BURNISHER in use in my young days (perhaps still used in England) was an oval piece of steel, tapering to a point, and set in a handle, burnisher and handle of about equal length, say five inches each. In America I found an ivory or bone paper-knife, slightly rounded at one end and nearly pointed at the other and sufficiently strong not to break easily, was in use instead of the burnisher, and I much prefer it.

A tiny morsel of ink being placed on any flat and hard

substance (you may as well get a square of plate glass or marble for the purpose), this is beaten by the ink-ball till the ink is thoroughly and evenly distributed. The least possible amount of ink should be taken at first, as any too much will over-ink the block, slurring fine exposed lines and filling fine incised lines. If the first impression be too grey, it is easy to take more ink for a second. Very little practice (and nothing but practice) will teach the right quantity. Beat the ball on the stone or glass, as hard as you like, to distribute the ink on the ball; but to distribute it from the ball to the engraving beat as gently as possible, not sparing of time. See that the ink is evenly spread over the whole surface. Then lay your paper, face downward, on the block, and hold it down with a thin card or piece of fairly thick smooth paper held in your left hand. This card or paper is to prevent the paper from slipping and so doubling the impression, and also to enable you to turn up portions of the India-paper from time to time, to see that the impression is perfect. Over this card (which also protects the thin India-paper) you rub the burnisher until you have got a clear print of every line. Sometimes in a darker part, or where there is a solid or sharp black, you may touch the back of the paper itself with the burnisher, to emphasize the part with directer pressure.

When proving a "vignette" (a subject with loose and light and scarcely defined edges), or a diagram or other outline subject, the broad masses of wood in the corners or elsewhere may be left standing, for the protection of exposed lines, till your proofs are taken. Cut a piece of thin paper to the shape of this standing wood (such protective piece is called a *frisket*), and after inking your block lay it on the same, to prevent it from being printed with your engraving. You may find it necessary to wipe off a portion of the ink from delicate edges and highly exposed lines, either with your finger or with a tongue of folded India-paper. Else they may come unduly heavy in the impression. Do not deceive yourself, nor attempt to deceive your employer, by producing in this manner an impression not fairly producible by your work !

If there are lowered parts, you will press your finger (not the burnisher) in to bring them up. Of such lowering nothing has yet been said, but it will be noticed presently.

I have said that proofs have to be taken, that the engraver may see the exact result of his work. In most cases, however, he may be content with blacking the block, with only ink enough to blacken it, not enough for printing. He should then be able to see what alterations are required. Never forget that wood-engraving is not susceptible of much amendment : do not trust then to after-work, nor calculate on final " touching." There is also a freshness and vigour in first work, which is in great measure lost by after-toning and correction, however necessary. Still some may be necessary. Let the engraver leave the blacked block for twenty-four hours before working on it. In that time the ink will harden and be less likely to be rubbed into the interstices, to the obscuring of his work. Having been so slightly blacked, the ink may be rubbed off the finished block with a piece of India-rubber (well to use that even before this first blacking, to get rid of any remaining ground, and of any grease from the hand) ; but when several impressions have been taken, the block may need washing with turpentine (never anything but turpentine) and a piece of woollen cloth. It

should then be set on edge to dry in a cool place, out of
the wind, to prevent warping. Of course such washing
blackens the whole block, after which no touching can be
done without filling between the lines with " whitening,"
a very disagreeable process and to be avoided.

It may be well to observe here that, to prevent warping, a block should be kept as much as possible in a mean
temperature, generally standing on its edge. If it warp
while on the sand-bag, counteract the tendency by placing
it face downward as soon as you leave off work. Well-
seasoned wood should not be liable to warp, if well cared
for.

Of LOWERED WORK.—Papillon first, and Bewick afterwards, used to lower the surface of light or much exposed
lines, in order that there might not be so much pressure
upon them in printing. When, some forty years ago, the
steam-press came into use (first, if I recollect rightly, for
the *Penny Magazine*), it was thought more than ever
necessary to have this protection, and not trust only to
printers' " overlays "—extra thicknesses of paper carefully
shaped so as to give gradated pressure on the different
parts of the block. Jackson or Chatto (*Treatise on Wood-
Engraving*) gives a long and particular account of this
lowering, assuming its advantages and necessity. It was
found, however, to fail in practice. The draughtsman,
having had a block carefully lowered according to his design, would change his purpose and, perhaps drawing a
solid block in a hollow, or a few light lines on a height,
entirely destroy the intended effect of the lowering. Also
the cutting upon a block much lowered was found to be
very awkward. Whether for these reasons, or other
economical ones, the practice was abandoned. Later,

working for the steam-press, for the *Illustrated London News*, I used to lower my blocks *after* the engraving was done : lowering and re-cutting such lines only that required to be more delicately rendered. I think it well that this should be done in exposed parts where less ink, as well as less pressure, is desired : though the object may be defeated by the printer, who has been known to knock up these lowered lines to the level of the others, from the back of the electrotype, now generally used instead of the block itself for printing from.

The lowering of lines will be done with the flat chisels, 11, 12, at page 38, the smaller used for inner parts of the block. The same smaller chisel will be found useful in cutting out, and, as it were, modeling the shapes of clouds.

# CHAPTER VII.

## OF THINGS TO BE AVOIDED.

 ARELESSNESS, inattention, irregularity, as they hinder progress in everything, so are things to be avoided even in the pleasant and easy occupation of engraving in wood. Self-conceit may be left on one side. And slovenliness and all other forms of indolence, even to the idle attitude of the young engraver below, may be avoided also. Avoid haste! It may be very important, doubtless, in a commercial sense, that an engraver should be quick; but there are two kinds of quickness,—the quickness of haste and the quickness acquired by the intelligent practice which enables the hand to be both ready and sure. "The more haste the worse speed" is a true proverb, and to nothing more truly applicable than to art. Certainly so, when the

artist is a learner; and it has been said by some one of
authority that the greatest artist never ceases to be that,
not caring to outgrow the advantage.   Learn to be quick
by learning to do well !   He who has, never so slowly,
learned thoroughly, has his brain prompt to direct, and for
action will, perhaps not in his earliest days, but surely in
due time, be a quicker workman than his unstudied
fellow.   Not quicker, perhaps, in his good work than the
other in his badness, though he may be that; but it is good
and not bad which is the object of teaching.   Enough,
however, of personal qualities, obvious to every one, of
whatever profession.   What are the special things to be
avoided in wood-engraving ?

Avoid broken black lines, unless purposely broken ;
rottenness of line, when part of the surface of a line is cut
away, or when the line is undercut, so that it breaks
down ; shallowness of cutting, so that the ink gets between
the lines, and hinders a clear impression ; unfinished work
—that is to say, lines in which the graver has stopped
short of intention or, beginning carelessly, has left a backward piece of wood only to be cut away by returning the
line ; and stops left in tints where, perhaps to obtain a
change of colour, a new line had been begun.   Avoid, also,
any unintentional light gaps in a tint (no matter what the
substance), resulting from too great pressure on the graver
or tint-tool, often from the too sudden change of line
where the same texture and tone are to be maintained only
slightly modified in colour ; and, at the same time, avoid
an absolute formality of line (except in machinery or
smooth and even surfaces)!   This coming in a sky may
sometimes, as the line regularly alternates between convex
and concave, occasion an appearance as of watered silk

(instead of the even tint desired), the convex lines, though cut with the same tool, and to the same precise depth as the concave lines, varying from them in colour, as a mere effect of light. These things will be soon perceived, and easily avoided by the engraver; but others may not so certainly claim his attention.

For one, let him avoid fine (minute) work in exposed places,—places with white around them,—where there is a tendency for the impression to dip, and make them heavy in colour. As a rule, it may be observed that a few thin *black* lines, standing closely together by themselves, are with very great difficulty printed delicately, and will show as an unsightly spot, even though lowered (as isolated and exposed lines always should be). Though the printer do his best, he can hardly, in such a case, prevent the too heavy printing.

Avoid fineness also in a foreground,—that is, undue fineness, undue as compared with the rest of the engraving. There is something of perspective even in the lines of an engraving. The background being free and open, too great minuteness in the foreground will look out of character, and will more or less unpleasantly deceive the eye. For the same reason, if the foreground must be treated minutely, the background should be correspondingly fine, or fair distances will not be kept. Avoid disproportion and incongruity !

Avoid slips, or miscutting, recollecting the small chance there is of mending a wood-engraving ! What is done is done. You may have to throw away your block, sacrificing all that is already done (engraving and drawing), if your error be serious ; or, even if it be slight, your only remedy is a piece of new wood let into the block, and so much engraved again, with a possibility that the piece let in may show. This letting-in of pieces to remedy mistakes is called " plugging." The best way of plugging is to drill a round hole in the block to about half its thickness, and then cut a piece of wood (with the grain) to the exact size, and hammer it in, making sure of its being quite tight, and at the same time careful not to split the block. If you need a large plug, a little of the very thinnest glue will be required to hold it firm. If your piece to be re-engraved is too large for a round plug, put in two, or three—in any case, only one at a time; and, if you have three, put in the centre one last, to help to tighten the others. You will cut the tops off the plugs nearly close to the face of the block with a penknife, or a fine saw (made of a watch-spring is the best), first cutting a hole the size of the plug in a piece of card, and putting the card round the plug on the block, to prevent accident to the surrounding parts. Then level the little wood left with your chisel. You may also glue a piece of wood to the side of your block. But all this plugging and joining supposes bungling, which had better be altogether avoided.

Avoid, except as mere experimental practice (which gene-rally had best be kept to yourself), all tricks and crotchets, such as new inventions of elaborate combinations of line, which may only show your own cleverness or eccentricity, without in any respect improving your work ! It is not the engraver that we wish first to think of in looking at an engraving ; and you may be sure, as a rule, that sim-plicity is better than elaboration. I allow that simplicity is more difficult, but difficulty does not deter the real artist. There is also a clever way of hiding want of knowledge under an affectation of much labour. It cheats the literary critic, who counts the number of lines and notes their intricacy, taking that as indication of excellence ; but it never deceives one who can judge of engraving. There is danger, too, that the satisfaction the pseudo-engraver takes in this display may so fill him with self-conceit, that he will disesteem and neglect the older simpler methods ; and once he begins to pride himself on his manipulation instead of on his art, he is, as an artist, lost. There is no recovery for such. The danger had better be avoided.

Not that I would discourage any attempt at discovery, nor insist that all the possibilities of art are exhausted, that the engraver should never stray from established bounds. I confess that I do not esteem all rules and regulations as absolute laws. But such principles of action as have been declared and exemplified by the masters of an art, have not been dictated merely by caprice. They have had some growth in observation and experience. Try all things, but hold fast to what has been generally received as good until you have some certainty of the equal or superior worth of your own conceit. Wait until your apprenticeship is over before you assume to teach your masters, and doubt your discoveries till you have come out of school ! This is only again saying, Avoid self-conceit ! And with some reference, also, to this kind of over-elaboration and fine intricacy, let me repeat, Avoid unmeaning lines ! Where one line will give good result, do not put two merely to have the credit of "fine" work ! Avoid obscurity, vagueness, uncertainty ! All these are signs of weakness : they show that you did not know what you were about. They are marks of the novice and the bungler, not of the artist.

# CHAPTER VIII.

## OF THINGS TO BE AIMED AT.

THE drawing you have to engrave may be an original design drawn on the block by the designer, yourself or another, or it may be the copy of some picture.

If the drawing be your own, and of your own designing, surely you know your own intention, and can have little hesitation as to the manner of treating it in engraving : that is, supposing you have carefully studied the different details of your art, have learned how to manage your graver, have obtained certainty of hand whether to cut a white line or to leave a black one to the form and size you desire ; and if you have learned also to estimate the relative value of lines in contrast with each other for expression of differences of substance, or of gradations of colour in your tints. These things mastered, you are qualified to engrave whatever drawing you are capable of making. Aim now at such combination of these things as will produce a perfect work : a work in which the parts accord, in which one part shall not, however well cut, be too coarse or too fine for another, in

which distances shall be preserved, colour attended to,
forms well defined, and (if the size of the subject allow
it) the differences of substance distinctly expressed. Care
for fitness and appropriateness in everything ! Do not
cut a sky with a rough line as if it were a piece of rugged
rock ; or a piece of broken ground or rock with a smooth
straight line, trusting only to colour to express unevenness.
Let your work also in its fineness or its boldness have
some reference to its size and to the subject represented.
You may be restricted in price, and know that your work
must be submitted to very ordinary printing : in that case
you will not treat even a small subject with minute elaboration, but (unless it be some microscopic or other drawing, in which minuteness of detail is necessary) you will
treat it simply and solidly, with firmly drawn lines, keeping your tints fairly distinct, and all except the darkest
rather under colour,—aware that common printing with
inferior ink can not render a tender gradation of tones, or
preserve either delicacy of outlines or purity of finer tints ;
that, in fact, all your greyer work, if really printed up
(which is always to be insisted on), will come darker than
in fine printing, and your darker tints so less distinct.

Again, if your subject be large, do not crowd it with a
multitude of lines, but let your engraving be large also,
bold and determined ! Nothing shows more the weakness
of an engraver than his fear of rendering large forms and
vigorous drawing with appropriate grandeur and force.
I am not desiring an engraver to be careful for opportunities of display ; but bidding him to fit his work to the
occasion, not to treat a design by Michael Angelo as he
would a Mulready or an Ary Scheffer. Of course the
grander design may be full of details, and to give all these

worthily may necessitate a smaller treatment ; but, to lay
down a rule, I would say,—Rather in all cases have your
work too large than too small.  The able engraver, sure of
himself, will only refine and work minutely when he sees
reason for refinement ; the less able, working in fear, will
not hide his weakness by elaboration.  Let him aim higher!
let him dare !  Let him rather fail from being too venture-
some (building honestly on the knowledge acquired by
conscientious study), than fail from meanness of purpose.
His failure in attempt will help him to a later success.
Aim always at strong and full expression ! through that
only will you reach the more subtle delicacy which is
truth grown beautiful.  Plain sense before poetry !  You
can not get poetry without,—nor the poetry of Art.  You
get only prettiness.

Independently of price paid, though not without reference to subject, the very size of an engraving will to
some extent dictate the manner of treatment.  (The question of payment for finer work need not disturb us here.)
For subjects in which minuteness of detail can not be avoided
—microscopic or less minute—the subject itself absolutely
determines the fitness of line.  But it is absurd and con-
trary to all artistic fitness to cover a large block, where
the forms are large and suggestive of breadth, with insig-
nificant lines, for no apparent reason but that the engraver
did not know his business, could not cut a sure line—a
line with meaning—and so sought to hide his incapacity
by the multiplicity of his scratchings.  An engraver should
know that there is a fitness of large or small work even
for the particular size of an engraving, with the exceptions
already noted.  Give me the same subject, landscape or
figures, to be engraved in three sizes ; surely I will not

treat all with the same strength of line, but I will cut
them according to size, the largest with bolder lines than
the smallest. If I well choose my lines, so that they are
most suitable for the size, my judgment will be found
correct when, photographing the same to the smaller or
the larger scale, the lines yet appear in accordance with
the subject, and as agreeable as at first. This sufficiently
condemns the misuse—which is waste—of labour in that
whole class of ultra-minute work in which engravers
foolishly compete one against another, for which publishers must pay, and which is ignorantly lauded by art
critics as " beautiful " *because many-lined.* Many-lined,
with each and every line of utter worthlessness. Our
laudatory reviewer has not found that out.

Aim at distinctness of expression in everything. Every
line should be chosen. When I look at an engraving of a
head, and find that the flesh is not distinguishable from
the hair, that part of a man's smooth cheek might be a
piece of cloth—being engraved in precisely the same line
as the cloth in the same engraving (an engraving large
enough to well represent varieties of texture), when I find
a hat (not of fur), hair, and immaterial (should be aerial)
background, all of the same substance, when I find an eye
formless, and a nose of wood or plaster, the shapes and
contours everywhere undefined and confused, I can but
say, despite the admiration of my friend the art critic, and
notwithstanding that I may acknowledge the fair general
effect of the head (before close examination), I can but say
very sorrowfully—Either this engraver had not learned how
to engrave, or, knowing how, he has been disloyal to his
art. I care not to ask the reasons for his disloyalty. I have
not to think of *him.* I can but condemn the *engraving.*

Or when I see a landscape, very excellent in colour and preservation of effect and general tone, nay, more, so carefully done, with such close attention to the picture from which it is copied, that you seem to see the very brush-marks on the canvas, but in which the sky is more woolly than a foreground sheep, and the sheep cut with precisely the same line as the water, and the water with the same line as the grass, what must be my judgment of this as *an engraving ?* An engraving is a picture represented by lines. Shall I call a picture represented by inappropriate, uncertain, inexpressive lines, a good engraving ? If there is no beauty in the lines, even only as lines, shall I call the engraving, which is only a representation by lines, a beautiful engraving ? The admiring crowd of ignorance and the literary art-judges pronouncing *ex cathedrâ* may call it so. I, as an engraver, can but condemn it for its inefficiency.

I am not supposing cases on which to build an argument. I am writing of two much-praised engravings lying before me as I write. Yes ! lying before me. They are not honest engraving.

Aim at distinctness of expression in everything ! Every line should be drawn—well drawn. The two cuts just criticized are copies from pictures, perhaps photographed on the block, and engraved therefrom. In having to copy the vague I find some excuse for the engraver's vagueness. But it seems to me that vagueness is as undesirable for the lover of art, as it must be unsatisfactory to the artistic engraver himself to be employed upon it. It is hardly to be expected that he shall engrave NOTHING with well-chosen lines. Perhaps NOTHING, however well painted, is unworthy of any lines whatever. I know there is a theory that an engraving should be like to a photographic rendering of the picture, " true " to the painter's faults, his vagueness, his brush-marks.   That is to say, true to the false, the inane, the unimportant.   I would agree to the unimportant, if not sacrificing the important. But it is a false theory that any art, even the very humble art of the engraver, should be so servile.   It ceases to be art when servile.   Your most excellent representer of brush-marks is not an artist, but at best a very skilful mechanic.   Would the painter himself, engraving his own picture, reproduce those brush-marks ?   He might, from utter ignorance of the technicalities of the engraver's art, or from more ignorant contempt of the special properties and excellences of engraving, be careless of rendering his picture with well-chosen lines ; but assuredly he would not be careful to exactly copy hasty or false drawing, nor would he waste his time in repetition of his hastiest and most careless handling.   Granted that an engraver shall take no liberties with the painter's work under his hands.   Alas for him, if he must follow the poorer artist !   Nevertheless an engraving is not, can not be a fac-simile of a picture, nor yet a photographic reproduction of it.   It is *a translation of colour into lines.* Hogarth, engraving from his own pictures, so treated them.   He never thought of them as merely paintings with the colour left out.   The engraver has to render colour in black and white lines.   Also, as one object of art is pleasure, his least important lines should not be unpleasing.   Of this again.

It may be that it is not the copy of a picture, but an original drawing on the block by the designer himself that is before you to be engraved.   To this you can not be too

faithful. It is no more a translation, but a reproduction
which you have to do. If it be a drawing in lines only,
you have to exactly keep those lines; if a drawing in
wash, you have to express the various shades and tints in
lines, keeping exactly to colour and form. Study well
and closely observe the peculiarities of style, that the
work may be seen at once to be by the designer, though
your own marks be only the distinction of excellence!
Certainly an engraver may have a style of his own; as
certainly it should not interfere with the style and character of the draughtsman. Efface yourself (not servilely),
because here you are not a translator, but a follower.
Here so much is not left to you as in copying a picture.
All is before you; the difference between a drawing in
black and white and an engraving is by no means so great
as between the engraving and the picture. But here, too,
some judgment and intelligence may be required of you,
beyond the mere choice of kind and direction of line.
That will be all if we assume that the draughtsman knows
thoroughly what can and what can not be done by the engraver. But he may not understand this, and then it is
within your province to set him right. If even in the
fac-simile drawing he has lines too close together in the
broader lights, not knowing, or forgetting, that the lines he
has drawn in grey will be printed black, it is for you to
correct that by substituting fewer lines of a similar character, true to the spirit, if not to the letter of his intention. If in his washed drawing he has chosen, as is often
done, to cover a tint with lines, you have sometimes to
choose between his lines and his tint, or to endeavour with
other lines to give the effect of his combination. Something will be left to your judgment in almost every drawing.

I speak here of drawings made on the block. When, instead of a drawing made directly on the block by the designer, you have only a photograph of some much larger drawing, or perhaps a careless and unfinished sketch, the claim upon your intelligence will be yet greater. The reduced sketch may be so little adapted for engraving that you are puzzled how to treat it at all. You can not make a satisfactory engraving without altering, completing, it may be, with your graver drawing—not re-drawing it, but putting it into a shape to be called a drawing. It does not follow that all sketches shall make so great a demand upon you. But in not a small proportion of your work, in picture-copying, or in engraving from sketches or drawings, you will find room for intelligence and artistic skill beyond the constant duty of invention of line.

And now one crowning work remains, one highest aim. Your ground or rock may be known without fear of mistake, your skies may be full of air, your clouds well rounded and as in motion, grasses and foliage may be shapely and natural, figures well formed, water well-drawn and liquid, textures of birds, or fish, or animals, or metal, or glass, or draperies, fairly distinguished,—everywhere your thoughtful line, not over-laboured, nor too mannered or conventional, but free and artistically expressive, may be most suitable to its purpose,—beside this you have kept a proper relation of fineness or boldness in your tints, and well noted distances for your perspective,—your general effect is complete: you have yet to aim at what I may call the linear harmony of all these things, the keeping of all lines not only in accordance with the shapes, and colours, and textures, of the separate parts of

the engraving, but also in harmonious relation one to
another (whatever the picture engraved) as they would be
in a beautiful face or figure. This brings us to the farther
consideration of what is meant by BEAUTY OF LINE. It is
fitness with an added grace.

# CHAPTER IX.

O UT of an impressionist school of painting, and subservient to the conditions of the impressionists, has arisen a school of impressionist engraving, the perfection of the imbecile. I find no other word so fit to characterize the process. The piece of work below is an exact reproduction (not enlarged) of part of a " cloudy sky " in a

*" Cloud."*

recent number of an art-paper. It may serve as text for our chapter upon BEAUTY OF LINE. I doubt not that the draughtsman with certain hasty washes of the brush drew in this sky in such carelessly impressive manner as is here apparent in the work of the engraver, whose lines perhaps have not unfaithfully followed even the directions suggested by the brush. Does any one think that the lines here given, however suggested or set in order by the artistic brush, are in any sense fit to represent a cloudy sky? Do they at all present it to us? In good engraving there must be always fitness of line. Good engraving is the forming of a picture by fit lines. And fitness of line will always lead to beauty. I can not think of a good engraving but as a work of beauty, a work of high art, however it may be disparaged by those without artistic knowledge to lift them to its comprehension.

The bit of "engraving" I give here is perhaps an extreme, but it is not an unfair instance of the kind of work which I have said has come into vogue through what is called the "Impressionist School" of painting. Some young men, lacking neither cleverness nor conceit, persuaded themselves that much labour, close study, and thoroughness, were not requisite. They made admirable sketches in colour, and thought them as good as finished pictures. The sketches were finished enough to give you a pleasant impression of the painter's intention; and what more could be desired? The world cares for sketches by the elder Titian: why should not the sketches of the younger Titian, just fresh from school, be cared for equally? Conceit is daring, and daring commands, when it may not deserve success. The young Titians forthwith set the fashion: they praised each other, crowed much, and friendly young art-critics joined in the jubilation. Let it be said that these impressionist painters, whose headquarters were of late in New York, may perhaps have

deserved praise for their departure from the hackneyed
ways of their elders; let it be admitted that their most unfinished paintings have all the merit claimed for them.
That does not concern me here. But it does concern me,
and concerns my teaching, that these same painters began
to draw for engravers, and to draw upon wood, and with
this sketchy work of theirs inaugurated "a new era in
engraving," the results of which may be best studied in
the two American magazines, *Harper's Monthly* and the
*Century*.

Our older draughtsmen on wood, the poorest as the most
talented, with very few exceptions, had all one virtue—
their drawings were careful. They were not sketches, but
drawings. A drawing on the block by W. L. Leitch (the
landscape painter), or by Duncan, was as beautifully complete, as carefully finished as a water-colour painting.
The drawings of Thurston and of Harvey were of the same
perfection. George Cruikshank's drawings were as clear
as his etchings, perhaps more precise. But the new men
have been, and are, disdainful of this drudgery. Yet,
with a strange inconsistency, while insisting that any hasty
and unconsidered sketch is good enough to be engraved
from, they require from the engraver a slavish adherence
to the slightest and most trifling accidents, and most
flagrant errors of their crude performances. From this
unsatisfactory pretence of drawing, coupled with the unfortunate use of photography, instead of drawing on wood,
has proceeded the present degradation of the art. Will
the art-critic open his eyes? Everywhere one hears it
said, authoritatively, and repeated, as if there could be no
doubt: "What a wonderful advance has been lately made
in wood-engraving!" I protest, unhesitatingly and

positively—If I know what engraving is, or should be, this vaunted "advance" must be condemned as retrograde, and as the degradation of the Art.

Here, by way of parenthesis, let me acknowledge the ability of both artists and engravers whose work I have to criticize. There are perhaps at this time in America as many artists who could draw on wood, and as many engravers capable of good work, as have been known in the art for the last fifty years. It is not the men I would attack, but the method of work they have adopted or submitted to. And when I refer to America especially, it is not that I recognize the "new" method as of American invention, but because in America has sprung up the claim to regard it as most excellent, and in the pages of the two magazines I have named, I find its most notable examples.

I have cared throughout all my teaching, and endeavoured in my practice, to insist upon the recognition of engraving as an art. I find nothing I can honestly call art in the "new departure" or "new development," by whichever name it may be known. I find a most marvellously successful mechanism, which is not an advance in *art*. Let my reader take any number of the *Century* or *Harper*, and try if he can discover (except in the portraits, and some few other cuts, I cannot remember many) *any lines that have beauty, or fitness, or any sign of intelligence.* Colour is kept admirably; delicacy—that is, fineness, thinness of line—is most remarkable; the often needless, sometimes unhappy, minuteness is astonishing. I am surprised at these accomplishments, often exceeding what I thought possible in wood-engraving. It is the triumphant assertion of mechanical skill. What eyes

these men must have! what nicety of hand! But
then ———

I have to speak as an engraver. In the prettiest and
most successful of these engravings I look in vain for anything to tell me that the engraver had any brains; that he
could have known or understood the forms he was engraving; that he had any thought of perspective, any perception of differences of substance. In nearly all the cuts the
foreground objects are on the same plane as those in the
background—there is neither air nor distance; sky may
be wall, and water may be folds of drapery, for any difference of treatment; and the lines throughout are laid with
utter disregard of the things to be represented by them, in
seeming ignorance or wilful rejection of all the laws of
linear beauty and perspective recognized and cared for by
the masters of engraving, both in wood and copper. The
horizontal lines of a sky are crossed perpendicularly; the
bark of a tree, a woman's cheek or bosom, a sheep's back,
have no distinction of line to denote difference of substance; foreground and distance are cut with the same
unvarying fineness; all things stick together; all things
are undefined, muddled, confused. Colour, I have said, is
excellently kept; and your first impression, not noticing
the lines, taking the picture only as a clever and very
exact imitation of a photograph, may strike you very
pleasantly; but if you return to it, if you examine it, you
will get no satisfaction from it. The enduring pleasure of
a beautiful engraving it will not give you. Forget the
lines altogether, it may be possible to like it; but you will
not care to look at it again and again. The more closely
you examine it, the greater will be your disappointment.
Does not that of itself condemn it?

Meanwhile, in the pages of these same magazines, there are portraits, engraved with full understanding and appreciation of the beauty of line, which by their juxtaposition only make the unredeemed ugliness of figure and landscape the more conspicuous. I can hardly over-praise some of these portraits. There are heads by Kruell and Johnson and Vellen which are of the best ever engraved in wood. The drawing is firm and definite; the flesh does not want for fleshiness; the lines are laid harmoniously, so that in themselves they are a delight to see. Why should this be thought necessary or worth doing in a portrait, and yet be altogether neglected or despised in everything else? I do not understand why this should be; but I know that the attention in one instance rebukes the neglect in the other.

The *laws of line* are not merely the pedantry of the schools. They have arisen out of the very nature of Art, and are as absolute and incontrovertible as any other of artistic principles. That a line—every line—should be beautiful is involved in the assertion that *Art is the expression of Beauty.* To say that a picture should be beautiful is but to say that it should be beautifully done. And however unaware we may be of the origin of those beautiful fitnesses of line which characterize the works of the greatest engravers; however conventional and arbitrary they may appear; nay, however mannered they may sometimes become in the formality of inferior practitioners, they are yet rules for our guidance, which we can not neglect or violate with impunity. Haste may excuse departure from them, as in the slighter studies of the great painters we see shadow lines put in merely as memoranda, scribbled in without heed or need of better forming. If the en-

graver, on whom I am desirous of impressing this law of
line, will for himself attempt, not a hasty sketch, but a
careful *drawing*, such as I will now suggest to him, he will,
I think, better understand the matter.  Let him draw a
hand, a finger, or only the end of a finger-bone !  Let him
draw it with lines only, fine lines, but quickly and freely,
with little or no scumbling !  The first line he draws (or
I am much mistaking) will be a circular line, some indication of the general shape.  Not perfectly accurate in
this, he will correct his line with other lines, also circular.
He will notice as he goes on, shadowing, and more and
more approaching toward completion, that, without any
thought on his part, the tendency and general direction of
his lines has always had relation to the form of the bone.
He will find in other trials that he can express form, con-
vexity or concavity, absolutely by lines, without colour.
The law here instanced rules everything.  In a tree or a
cloud, as also in the beautiful lines of mountain form, the
same law obtains.

And now consider that an engraving is *a picture produced
by lines*—an engraving in wood producible *by lines only*—
and that you can not get rid of the lines.  You can not cut
lines so fine that they can not be seen.  Is it not well, therefore, that what must be seen should be as agreeable as
possible ?  Is it not clear that, as you use only lines in
your work, the more these lines indicate or express, the
more complete and satisfactory will be your work ?  Shall
they not, even by their direction, rather explain, or help to
explain, the shape or substance you have to represent with
them, than distort or hide it ?  Why, then, in the photo-
graph-imitations of the *Century* and *Harper* have you abandoned all thought of what is valuable in line, its artistic

use ? If you choose to care most for colour—chiaro-scuro rather—still does that necessitate an absolute disuse of line ? For in the cuts I condemn, lines are not used, they are only put up with : their real use is avoided. Instead of caring for their use and beauty, you seem to have cared rather to make them injurious and offensive. Let us have photographs at once, with all their indefiniteness and obscurity—let us have reproductions by any process which has not lines—but let not artistic taste be insulted and outraged by lines deliberately opposed to beauty, in every respect unfit for the purpose for which they should be chosen !

In thus contending for a beautiful fitness of line as *a primary and most important element in engraving*, I am not underrating colour and tone. Neither in insisting on the value of such examples of linear beauty as have been given us by the greater masters, am I forbidding the employment of new and improved manipulation. I am contending against an exclusive attention to colour ; and insisting only *that lines shall have meaning*—that it shall not be matter of indifference whether they are suitable or not. Let the engraver mimic brush-marks, if he can find reason or occasion for doing so. I find fault in him, not for caring for the unimportant, but for forgetfulness or wilful neglect of the important. Let him bring his sackful of mint and anise, if he will so burden himself, but not make it a plea for despising the higher law ! I am not so unreasonable or unpractical as to ask an engraver to treat two substances of different texture with characteristic difference of line where, from the necessary minuteness of work, he has no fair opportunity for such distinction. Always provided that the minuteness is necessary, and not merely adopted

as an excuse for monotony. Also, supposing him to perceive some value in line, I shall not ask him to follow
Sharp, or Warren, or Milton, or Pye, or other of the great
copper-engravers, capable of teaching him, but leave him
to invent, if he can, a more expressive system for himself.
Let him have a line of his own, and over-rule the rules of
all who have preceded him. I will even refrain from blame,
though sorry and surprised, if he seriously tell me that
this new confounding all distinctions of substance in one
mechanical inexpressiveness affords the best scope for the
intelligent expression of differences. But even then I
would beseech him, though he prefer to have no differen-
tial intelligence in his line, at least to care a little for
some pleasantness of beauty,—at the same time confessing
that I have not much faith in beauty without intelligence.

I know that much may be done with a single line, a line
of only varying strength across the whole block. I may
be credited with having myself essayed this. Yes ! but, I
hope, not with a line without meaning. And such treatment is exceptional, not to be taken as a precedent for
universal practice. The exception really proves the rule.

But this opposing argument comes before me, from the
advocates of the " new departure." " If we have not been
careful for this expressiveness of line in the direction for
which you contend, it is because we have cared for it in
other directions. If we have not cared to cut a stone to
look like a stone, or to distinguish smoke from wool, we
may pride ourselves in showing from what our engravings
have been copied. When we engrave from a painting we
make that apparent, even to the brush-marks and touches
of the palette-knife; when we have a crayon drawing we
imitate the peculiarity of crayon; who can mistake our

engravings after the photograph ? " and so on.   Again I
say, it is care for the less instead of the more important.
Again I ask, if the painter were his own engraver, would
he reproduce his brush-marks ?   If the crayon-draughts-
man were an engraver, copying his life-size head (say of
Emerson) on a page of the *Century*, would he care to make
it look like a crayon-drawing ?   And, farther, I can not
find that these endeavours at imitation of other processes
have even the "justification" of success.   Your crayon-
like engraving will never pass for a crayon-drawing with
even the poorest of connoisseurs.   It will be only a literary
critic who will compliment you on your imitation of the
painter's handling.   You can not make an engraving look
like a painting after all.   And when you plume yourself
on the excellent " realism " with which you have rendered
the bronze or clay of a statue, may I not fairly ask you
whether that does not approve the justice of my contention ?   Take the foolish feather from your cap !   You can
only express that difference between bronze and clay by a
purposed alteration of line ; you are immediately forced
for the special occasion into the intelligent conduct which
you refuse to adopt for your general engraving.   I am not
admitting your success in these odd doings, failure for the
most part as is the mimicry of crayon and the brush.   And
the reason for failure is obvious.   Out of a general practice of unintelligent work you can not at any given
moment step into the circle of intelligence.   No less this
"realism," claimed as a special and new-invented grace of
the unintelligent development, this *realism upon particular
occasions* proves my case.   If you ought to express the
material of your statue, if it be well to distinguish between
bronze and clay in the engraving of only a statue, what

reason have you for refusing to express the difference when bronze and clay are parts of your engraving? It seems to me that in the general subject (where there is room for the expression) it is yet more important to express material. In the engraving of only a statue, if I have the perfect beauty of form, I may little care to know whether it is in bronze or clay, in marble or in wood; but in a general engraving I do care (so far as the size of the engraving will permit) to see this distinction of substance. I do care to see a tree, as in one of Milton's Irish views, so distinguished that every line of the drawing helps to inform me of its character. I am not content with what I get from my unintelligent engraver, " This is a tree, I can not tell you of what sort."

I may seem to be travelling out of my subject, the *beauty* of line. Nevertheless, in insisting on a truthful line—on at least a recognition—so far as always-imperfect practice will allow, of the advantage of truthfulness in engraving, that is, the choice of such lines as are fit for the purpose of pictorial representation by lines, I am ever referring to the one only basis of all beauty, which is truth.

Ask me to accurately define what beauty is, I confess that I can not. I can but point to examples. Look at free tree-growth, the natural untrained interlacing of the boughs and twigs; examine a bird's wing, and note not only the outer form and inner central line of each feather, but also the arrangement of lines throughout; remark that same beautiful line of the feather and the wing—the line ever departing from the confined circle, in all mountain form (if your good fortune ever carry you to the glorious mountain districts of our island); watch from any of our shores the play and change of line in the stirred waves; or at

your own hearth observe the varying forms of flame! You
will then see, if your eyes are not without vision (for the
eye sees only what it brings the means of seeing, and there
are who have eyes, yet see not) *what the lines of beauty are,*
and learn something of those underlying principles on
which, consciously or unconsciously, the lines of great
artists have been founded.

From Nature you may go to Art, and from Art return
again and again to Nature; and, once able to perceive
these lines, you will never again be content without
attempting to reproduce them in your engraving.

Let me caution you on one point, which may be necessary since I have referred you to copper-engravers for
examples *of line.* I do not want you to attempt *in black
line* what is so done by the copper-engraver. I think that
even our great engraver, John Thompson, for all his
mastership, lost sight here of the true principle of work
in wood—the white line of Bewick. But for *that white
line* we may most advantageously consult the black line
of the best engravers in copper. It is in the incised lines
of our white-line work that our *process* becomes identical
with theirs. In this white-line alone we are able to show
the full capability of wood-engraving; in this alone we can
fully earn the distinctive name of Artists.

# CHAPTER X.

### OF THE USE AND ABUSE OF PHOTOGRAPHY.

THE use of Photography as an adjunct to Art has been very great. But Photography can not take the place of Art, and Art can not be the mere imitation of a photograph.

Here are some of the supposed advantages of photography *as a substitute for drawing on wood*, the matter which immediately concerns us here. I take them from a writer who is convinced that " we owe the *improved* character of our wood-engraving more to that than to any other cause."

1. " It admits of the reduction of a drawing to a block of any desired size, and a freer handling so obtained,— drawing on the limited surface of a block having always been regarded by artists as a cramped business, the freest handling not attainable that way."

I answer :—Any good draughtsman can make a correct reduction to any desired size : correct as the photograph in proportions, more correct than the photograph as to effect in the copy of a picture. The supposed impossibility of free handling on the smallest blocks is disproved by

the works of Thurston, Harvey, Cruikshank, without need
of naming others, German, English, French, and American.
No freer handling can be found anywhere than in drawings
on blocks sometimes not more than an inch square ; nor
did the artists I refer to ever regard drawing for engravers
as " a cramped business." If drawing on the scale required for wood-engravers be cramped, what is engraving?

2. " It enables the engraver to have the original drawing always in front of him to refer to : no longer exposed
to the danger of losing general effect for want of anything
to compare with to keep the effect before him."

I answer :—The original drawing or picture may as
easily be had before the engraver whether his copy is
drawn on the block or photographed. And if it be a drawing on the block (only that, and nothing to refer to) he has
no need of anything but that drawing, in order to keep the
effect.

3. " It does away with the possibility of the design
being lost by an accident to the surface of the block while
the engraver is at work upon it."

I answer :—The provision is against an unheard-of
accident. Were it a common accident, it would be equally
provided against by a photograph *from* the drawing on the
block.

4. " It has the very salutary effect of making the engraver responsible to the artist for the effect he attains.
Before photography *upon wood* was adopted, an engraver
could say, when confronted with defects in his block,
' Your artist drew it so ! ' Now art-editors who give out
drawings upon the wood take the precaution to make
ferrotypes or negatives of them, so as to hold the engraver
to account if his work be unfaithful."

I answer:—The engraver is and always has been responsible to the artist, who can not so forget his drawing: that his word would not outweigh the excuses of an inefficient engraver. Very well that art-editors, publishers, and draughtsmen, should preserve photographs in case of the presumed dispute ; but photographs *from the drawings on the block* would answer the same purpose. There is no argument or reason for using photographs *on* the block.

5. " As an engraver goes over the surface of his block he destroys the drawing by transforming it into lines, which are actually meaningless and invisible until he blackens them with his lead pencil or ink-ball. He has to depend too much upon his memory, and he invariably loses and incurs the danger of substituting his own ideas for those of the artist. With the design *photographed upon the wood,* he has constantly before him the artist's work, and is really elevated, in a measure, into the position of an interpreter of it, a translator of it into a new medium. It is in this sort of inspiration of the engraver that the chief provocation to excellent work lies, because it conceals the mechanical aspect of his function as much as possible, and brings him into a more intimate and sympathetic relation with the artist."

I observe :—If an engraver is at work on a fac-simile drawing, in which alone exactness of rendering line for line (skilfully or rudely mechanical) is required, the supposed destruction of lines would be of no consequence. The line once cut is done with : the engraver may go on to the next without care for that already cut. There are no relations to keep, each line speaks for itself. Even if the engraved lines become invisible (*which they do not*), it would not matter. If he is foolishly impatient to see how he has cut a portion of his work, there is nothing to prevent him from amusing himself by blacking it with pencil. I should scold an apprentice for so wasting his time. Engravers, it may be added, do not invariably lose their drawing.

Secondly, if the drawing on the block is a washed drawing, it is not destroyed by being transformed into lines, nor is the effect of the work invisible or meaningless. A clean-handed and careful engraver (and even for the sake of finding use for photography an engraver need not be careless or dirty) will not rub out or lose his drawing, provided it is a properly made drawing on a fair ground, and he need not incur any danger of " substituting his own ideas." The relative colour of all parts of the engraved work will be clear to him, and little experience will enable him to allow for the somewhat lighter appearance of what is cut, as the white wood shows through the tint upon the surface. For the rest, the fifth "advantage of photography " may stand as fair sample of the acuteness of a literary art-critic.

I know of no other advantages claimed for the use of *photography on the wood.* Only some of the remarkable phraseology I have quoted remains for notice.

I am perhaps not gifted with sufficient intellect to appreciate the phenomena of elevation, inspiration, and provocation to excellence of work owing to having the drawing constantly before me *in the guise of a photograph instead of having the drawing itself.* To put this into other words, let us say that Gilbert or Duncan, in fac-simile or wash, has made a drawing *on the block*, and I have a photograph from this *upon another block.* Can anyone, except

an art-critic, suppose that I can gain in "inspiration," or
"provocation to excellence," through having the photograph instead of the original drawing given to me to engrave from ; that my position as interpreter or translator
will be in any way " elevated," or that the mechanical
aspect of my function (whatever that may mean) will be
concealed by the substitution of the photograph, and I be
so brought into " a more intimate and sympathetic relation with the artist " ?

I turn from the art-critic's words to the opinion of one
of the best of our engravers in wood, who also has had
wider opportunities than most of us for judging of engraving and for knowing the opinions and practice of engravers,—my friend, Mr. A. V. S. Anthony, of Boston. I
take from him a single statement which seems to me to
more than counterbalance all the advantages claimed for
photography, even if those advantages were established.
His statement is that " the engravers do not like engraving photographs, as, involving glances now and then at the
originals, it is ruinous to the eyes, which are unable to accommodate themselves to the changes of focus ; *and many
of the best men have been obliged to suspend work and seek
medical aid in consequence.*" My own hearing from engravers in New York is to the same effect. If this occurs
under the bright skies and in the clear atmosphere of
America, will it not be well to take warning here ? But
the man is sacrificed to the work. Shall not the artist
submit to blindness, a martyr for the improvement of his
art ? Is his art improved ? I have said, and hold to it,
that the supposed " improvement " is not improvement,
but degradation; the " advance " is, at best, crab-like,
one-sided, if not backward. Most wonderful delicacy of

tones has been obtained (not altogether new, but let that pass !): we will credit the " new departure " (which the art-critic is quite right in attributing to photography) with this delicacy. Has it not been attained by the sacrifice of force and definition ? Yet more wonderful fineness, with or without delicacy, is now the universal custom ; the universality is what is new. And the fineness, *which is not finish or refinement,* is not an improvement, but a hindrance to good. This—I say distinctly—is the result of the use of photography instead of drawing on wood.

Thurston, or Cruikshank, or Gilbert, in drawing on the wood (I speak now more especially of fac-simile) drew always with some thought of the engraver. Despite the asserted impossibility of free handling in so limited a space, they did draw freely, adapting their treatment to the size of their block, guided by their knowledge of the capabilities of engraving. Now the artist-designer seldom troubles himself about even the possibilities of engraving ; he makes his drawing, most easily for himself, on a large scale, in firm lines, or charcoal or loose chalk, as suits him : and this is reduced by photography to such size as may be desired for the book or magazine. Though his drawing be in the plainest possible lines, they have no reference to the size of the *engraving.* Lines not too fine or too numerous for the original may be too fine for the smaller size ; the loose chalk-dots clear enough in the larger work may be almost lost in the reduction. Instead of the thoughtful consideration of old time, we have now at best only a calculation, and in most cases not so much as a calculation, of how the drawing may appear in the photograph. And add to this that a photographed line is never so definite or distinct as even a grey line drawn in pencil. The critic knows nothing of all this; but every engraver does. There is sufficient reason for the engravers' dislike for the use of photography *instead of drawing.*

Again, we will consider the photograph on the block of a landscape or a figure subject direct from nature or from life. I do not here inquire if this is art; but is it of any advantage to the engraver? A photograph either takes in every detail sharply or loses details in the general massing of the effect. If the first, the picture on the block will be overcrowded with small forms beyond the possibility of graver-rendering. If the second, the details not sharp, the whole photograph is blurred and vague. Between inexpressive vagueness, and the impossibility of expressing a microscopic minuteness, the engraver loses himself. Opportunity for the first faculty of an artist— the understanding and expression of form—is denied to him. He is left with colour only. He becomes a mere representer of indefiniteness ; and represents it consistently with unmeaning dots and lines, and crossings of lines— the result a hotch-potch of shapelessness and unintelligibility ; his engraving—which should be a picture of forms and perspective and colour—having colour only. The photograph had no more : he was not called upon to better his instruction.

And, as some stress has been laid on the disappearance of lines when cut, let it be observed that, though this does not happen in drawings on wood when ordinary care is used, it does happen with photographs, which no care can preserve. All is lost as cut ; and the engraver may well need a second photograph, or the original of the one he works on, to help his memory.

Photographing on wood will *save the time* of the draughts-man, when a reduction of a drawing or a picture is wanted. If you must have the lines of the larger fac-simile drawing, you can only get them by photography. Use it then! but you will not escape the disadvantages I have noted. If you would have the best copy of *a picture,* do not be content with a photograph! The "correctness" of photography is a mistake. It is never correct. It always alters colours, and more or less disturbs effect, beside the before-mentioned overplus of detail. The artist-copier *translates* the painting into black and white, so making a truer copy than the photographer's ; and he puts on the block only what he knows can be engraved, helping the engraver by saving him the unpleasant and dangerous task of leaving out. Let the draughtsman economical of time have the picture—especially a portrait—photographed on the block, and then draw his translation over that. The engraver will be grateful to him.

It may not be uninteresting here to give account of the origin and occasion of this photographic usage, which was certainly not invented for the benefit of engravers.

It was invented by or for artists who could not draw on wood. There is a special faculty required for small drawing, as there is for fine engraving, gem-cutting, or other minute work. The sculptor may not be able to cut a cameo ; the painter of life-size figures may not be able to draw with the precision of a Gavarni or a Meissonier. Also, it has to be said, there are painters who can not draw at all. Other artists, who could draw, discovered that it would take no more time in designing, sometimes less time in drawing, if their works were on a larger scale. These photographed on the block, they could retain the originals, for which a market was open. So they were twice paid for their works, the publisher sometimes made a saving, the engraver was not cared for. From newspaper work, the new system spread to book-work; and, following on a long cheap system of careless fac-simile—fairly exemplified in early numbers of *Punch* and in the mass of engravings under the name of Dalziel (yet by no means confined to them)—gave the death-blow to engraving *as an art*. When a block the size of a page of the *Illustrated London News* or the *Graphic* was cut from a photograph on the block—the photograph of a slovenly sketch with superabundance of discordant and meaningless lines and confusion of tints, a sketch not intended for engraving,—when engravers, covering this to preserve it from destruction (for at the first these photographs faded away when exposed to the air), were obliged to work piece-meal, without the least understanding of what they engraved (the little uncovered bit might be a cloud or a door-mat, or anything else), the absence of anything like artistic work was sure. This is the way in which photography on wood came into vogue. This is the mission it has fulfilled.

The fading of the photograph has been remedied. And now at least the engraver can see his whole subject at once, a manifest advantage, being some help toward the comprehension of it. And in America, on the *Century Magazine* (originally *Scribner's*) and on *Harper's Monthly* engravers of talent found employment. But the objections to the use of photography, which I have been careful to note, remain the same. The most talented engravers are hampered and crippled by it; they are confined to colour, and compelled to indefiniteness; and they waste their powers on an excess of fineness, which may find ignorant admirers, but of which they themselves are ashamed. The end of this can be only imbecility in engraving, and then the substitution of some process for the mechanical weakness of the hand. For the mechanic-engraver the days of engraving are numbered. Only the artist-engraver, while he upholds the dignity, can assure the future of engraving. Beware of photography !

Two " Feet."
*Unintelligent work enlarged.*

## CHAPTER XI.

OTWITHSTANDING all that has been already said of the indispensable qualifications of an artist, I may venture on some farther words, to clinch what I have been hoping to drive into the minds of my readers desirous of learning the art of engraving in wood.

Let it not be thought contradictory if I again remark that an exact boundary-line between skilled mechanism and art is hardly to be obtained. The mechanic may have in himself, and express in his work, so much of taste and understanding that we dare not absolutely deny him the name of artist. The acknowledged artist may do what seems only mechanical, and yet in that give evidence of his artistic quality. There is no such thing as absolutely distinct classification. We can but classify broadly, admitting exceptions. Bearing this in mind, we may take extremes to illustrate our argument.

Here are two specimens of purely mechanical work : The *clean* cutting is by a skilled workman. The lines of themselves speak for him. They are true. He has cut them as drawn. We can but take his word, or this his mark, as sufficient evidence that the draughtsman so drew them. The *unclean* cutting is the work of an unskilled workman, or the unskilful work of the workman whatever his capacity. He can not make us believe in the truth of this work. No man could have drawn the lines as they appear here. He, the "engraver," perhaps did not even see the lines drawn for him. Anyway he did not see their importance, or of common honesty he would not have thought it enough just to cut out pieces of wood without any care for shape, so distorting every line of the drawing.

*Clean.*　　　　　　*Unclean.*

There may be no great evidence of skill even in the *clean* work, but there is proof of conscientious care, which is the beginning of skill. But the *unclean* shows plainly one of two things, ignorant incapacity, or (if the "engraver" were capable of better work) careless want of conscience. Unhappily, even in these days of "improvement" and new "development," the *unclean* still predominates, no cleaner because cut with a graver, and done so finely, so minutely as to appear quite excellent in the eyes of a critic satisfied with general effect, and unable to judge of accuracy or veracity.

Here is shown the difference between good and bad work of the simplest mechanical character. Let us look now at two examples of the difference between unskilful mechanism, however honest, and the skilled work which approaches to if it is not artistry. The cut beneath is an honest rendering of a drawing by Stothard in pen and ink. No drawing could be more plain. The lower, also from Stothard, from a draw-ing of precisely similar charac-ter, was engraved by Clennell. Two pieces of mere fac-simile, yet how differently cut! The one nothing but mechanism, the other (though we may only *class* the work as me-chanical) full of intelligence

and taste, evidently the work of an artist. It is the same excellence which we admire in the cuts by Lützelburger in the *Dance of Death.* So I would show how the lines of the highly-skilled " mechanic " run close to those of the " artist." Knife-work in one instance, graver-work in an-

other; that does not matter. The tasteful and skilled me-chanic is of the artist's family.

And in even so simple sub-jects as these Stothard cuts, where the wood is merely cut away so as to leave intact the clear—one would think un-mistakable—lines of a pen-and-ink drawing, we see the artist's superiority, and learn what constitutes an artist. Shall we say that every line of Stothard's drawing is given

by each of his engravers? It is not so. The one has
not given a single line of Stothard's drawing. He has
honestly, to the best of his unperceiving mechanical
ability, left a line wherever Stothard drew one. He saw
a line, and meant to preserve it; but could not, for he
never saw *what the line was*, never knew the value of
it. Eyes that saw not! So he has given us his own
woodiness in place of Stothard's free pen-and-ink. The
higher perception is what first goes to constitute an artist.
Also here may be learned what constitutes the beauty of
line. Every line of Clennell's work has beauty. There is
the same difference (it is the difference between lines without
form and lines with form, the difference between the unintelligent and the intelligent) in the cutting of a white line.

Or look at Branston's engraving (our frontispiece).
Here the drawing of the figures and some portions more
were, I believe, made in lines by Thurston; the rest, perhaps, in wash, with not more than direction of lines
marked. But the engraving is not mechanical. Admirably as Thurston, an accomplished copper-engraver, could
draw, with all the sharpness and fineness of an engraving,
Branston used his own intelligence. We do not see an
absolute adherence to the draughtsman's lines (as was
necessary in the Stothard autographs), but judgment in
taking advantage of his guidance. For the rest, the work
is Branston's own (nothing lost of Thurston), and more in
the manner of the "black-line" of copper-plate, as would
be natural from such a drawing, than in Bewick's "white-
line" manner; but with a mixture of both. The same
mixture is characteristic of Thompson's work, who also
preferred the manner of copper-plate; see the engraving
by him, also drawn by Thurston, on our title-page. In his

knowledge of effect—what I may call the perspective of his work—the placing of everything in its right place (it is worth while to compare anything of his with the present photographic fashion), in the firmness and decision and propriety and beauty of his line, John Thompson stands without a rival,—notwithstanding my unqualified assertion of Bewick's "white-line" as the true and more effective method of engraving in wood. Bewick was incomparably the greater artist; but, as *engraver only,* Thompson far surpassed him. I want to make this matter quite clear. Bewick and Clennell were masters of design and drawing —artists entirely independent of their work as wood-engravers; therefore, whatever they did upon wood would have an artistic quality, however carelessly or with technical inefficiency engraved by them. On the other hand, Thompson was not, so far as I am aware, at all distinguished, either as designer or draughtsman; but he had an artist's taste, and was perfect in his mastery of the graver. We never find a weak or badly placed line in the work we know to be by his hand. Do not think that is only mechanical at any time. In his work, as in Branston's, the line is his own. It is always a line drawn with the graver (except, of course, in merest fac-simile): in white line, indeed, though the result as seen, and as intended, is a series of black lines, while, in Bewick and Clennell, it is the white lines we are desired to see.

And here I join issue directly with our great etcher, Mr. Seymour Haden, who, in a sweeping condemnation of copper-engravers, seems to ignore altogether the artistic quality of their work, and, consequently, of that of wood-engraving also. I find him writing (*About Etching,* Part I., Note 5) :—

" The burin line, being without either originality or personality, is without mental expression, except *such little* as may be evolved from it in the act of copying."

The burin (graver) line of Bewick or Thompson without originality or personality ! Has any line of the etcher, Haden or Rembrandt, any greater originality, personality, or mental expression ? Is there no personality involved in the choice of a fit line, no mental expression in the enriching of lines even drawn by a Thurston ? Some originality may be at times when the engraver would represent a substance for which the conventional order of line (which, I suppose, is what Mr. Haden chiefly aims at) gives him no sufficient precedent. May I (and not immodestly) refer to the *Fruit* here opposite (my own work, part of a large engraving), as having so much of originality and personality as to indicate mental expression ? The draughtsman gave me no lines, nor hint of any. They are my own (personal), invented (that is originated) by me, the result of some thought and consideration (therefore not without mental expression). I claim again so much for the portion of a *Landscape* here next given. The lines in these two cuts, and in the portrait of *Whitman* (this last my own drawing from a photograph), are entirely my own. In the first two the work is all in "white-line;" in the portrait also, all except the few black lines in the principal lights. Does Mr. Haden mean to assert that a line cut with a graver, with forethought and intention, and chosen as most expressive, is less original, or less artistic, than an etched line ? It would be a poor quibble (which Mr.ˑ Haden would ˍnot make), because a line is *driven*, rather than *drawn*, by the graver-plough, that the line can not be as free. The graver may not be so easy to handle as the

*W. J. Linton, Sc.*

pencil, the pen, or the etching-needle ; but I do not find
that increased difficulty subtracts from artistic merit, or
that it alters artistic quality. A mechanic does not
become an artist by taking up an etching-tool, nor is he
less an artist if he use a graver. The artistry is in the
man, not in the tool; and as notable a lack of originality,
personality, and mind, can be pointed out in the lines of
fine etchings (so-called) as ever can be laid to the charge
of users of the graver, whether upon copper or on wood.

Mr. Haden appears to qualify his words with " except
such little as may be evolved in the act of copying." I
do not quite understand this : since the engraver from a
picture is not *only a copier*, but a translator. To borrow
some well-written words, criticizing the etcher's statement—

" Mr. Haden thus admits, if he underrates, the originality of the engraver's art. A painter interprets what he
sees in Nature or in imagination with his brush, his translation being from round into flat forms. An etcher does
the same, with the limitations implied in the absence of
colours, translating into the lines and dots of the etching
needle. The engraver interprets forms, colours, and
shadings of the brush, or some graphic instrument, into
the line or dot of the burin. There is as absolute a quality
of originality, however greatly it may differ in degree, in
one process as in any of the others. That involved in engraving may be more subtle, but it is no less genuine
than in painting or etching."—(*F. Seymour Haden and
Engraving.* Boston, 1882.)

I perfectly agree with this : always admitting that the
mere slavish copying or the unintelligent rendering of a
line, whether it be done with the graver or the etching-

needle, is not art. And I deny that etching, with its too facile employment of *any lines for colour*, and its tempting opportunities for evading definition and form, can take rank *as artist work* (that is, work of originality, personality, and mental expression,) above the "white-line" graver work of wood-engraving. I need not add a word for the great works in steel or copper.

Enough has perhaps been said to show what I consider is rightfully to be called artistic work : the capacity to execute which, in any material and with any tools, does, to my thinking, entitle the worker to the name of artist.

---

Yet, at the risk of repetition, a few more words on the wonderful fineness of late engraving in wood. Here I may be allowed to quote what I wrote, concerning this accomplishment of the "new departure," in the *Atlantic Monthly* for June, 1879. Continued observation of the exploits of the "departure" have not altered the judgment I then expressed.

As to fineness, it is altogether a mistake to suppose that a work can not be too fine, or that *fineness* (closeness and littleness of line) and *refinement* (finish) are anything like synonymous terms. There is such a thing as propriety— suitability, not only to size but to subject—in the treatment of an engraving. A work may be bold to the verge of what is called coarseness, yet quite fine enough for the purpose : by which I do not at all mean the purpose of the publisher, but the purpose of the artist. Also, it may be finished and refined, however bold : in which case to call it coarse, simply because the lines may be large and wide apart, would be only misuse of words. It is no proof of

judgment, when a publisher counts his lines, and thinks
there are too few for his money ; nor is it to the credit of
the engraver, when he endeavours to hide his ignorance of
drawing under a multiplicity of cross-hatchings, machine
or hand work equally false, so assisting at the farther de-
pravation of his employer's taste, and aiding and abetting
in cheating the innocent buyers of " illustrated" books into
a belief that the work is *fine*. Fine, indeed, in a finical
sense, but not fine artistically.

By such fineness a work is not bettered. The fineness
may be out of character with the subject, may positively
contradict its sentiment and manner. Think of Michael
Angelo's " Sybil " so finely (finically) engraved ! Has
one no instinct of impropriety there ? Or take some
landscape strong in opposition of colour, a wild, tempes-
tuous scene, large and vigorous in treatment ; the painter
has flung his paint upon it, left the coarse marks of his
half-pound brush and the mighty sweep of his trowel.
He cares not for that, need not care ; seen at a proper
distance the effect is what he desired. What would you
say to the engraver who should so far disregard the bold
carelessness characteristic of the painting, as to give you,
in niggling minuteness, every brush and trowel mark, in
order that, or so that, you may forget the real worth of
the picture, despite the painter's slovenliness and absolute disdain or dislike of finish, in your admiration of the
engraver's most delicate and neatest handling ? " See
how grandly broad the rendering of that cloud ! " (It is
perhaps the painter who speaks, talking to himself; or is
it the accomplished literary critic discoursing before the
picture upon matters of unknown art to an admiring
crowd ?) " A momentary sketch ! instantaneous as a

photograph! exceedingly effective! No, it could not be
improved by any additional care in modelling, or by any
gradations of shade or colour." Says the engraver, or his
work for him: "Never mind the cloud, or anything else
of the picture! See how admirably I have imitated the
crossing of the brush strokes; examine that bit of clotted
hair! Notice the shadows of the blobs of colour left where
the palette-knife laid it on! You can tell at a glance
which is brush-done and which is knife or trowel work."
Is that the purpose of engraving? Labour, even skilled
labour, can be ill-bestowed. And if, after all this trouble
about brush-marks, you have lost what drawing there
was in the picture, missed the very spirit and grandeur
of the landscape while busied with those little sprigs of
mint and anise in the corner, how shall your engraving
be called *fine*, though it needs a microscope to enable me
to count the lines? What wonderful eyes! What dexterity of hand! But after all it is *not a fine engraving*.
Fine, as an artist's word, is not the same word as in the
proverb of the feathers. Fine feathers may make fine
birds, but fine lines will not make a fine engraving. The
one is the French *fine*, thin, crafty, not exactly honest:
from which are many derivatives, such as *finasser*, to use
mean ways; *finasseur*, a sharper; *finasserie*, petty trick,
poor artifice; *finesse*, cunning, &c. Quite other is the
masculine *fin*, the essential, from which we get *finir*, to
finish, and *finisseur*, a finisher or perfectioner. And the
first *fine* is the very opposite of the old Roman *finis*, the
crowning of the work. The artist does care for finish,
that is the perfectness of his work; he is below the real
artist and will reach no greatness whenever he can be content with the *unfinished*. But the word *fine*, the proper ad-

jective for a great work, was taken, perhaps unaware, by
poor engravers, careful mechanics without capacity for
art, as a cover for their deficiencies, and, accepted by
ignorant connoisseurs, now passes current for the beguile-
ment of trusting publishers and an easily bewildered
public. So trick is admired instead of honest art workmanship. An engraving is *fine*, that is *good*, so far as art,
as distinguished from mechanism, has been employed
upon it, and is visible in the result : visible, I would say
farther, even to the uneducated, if not already vitiated by
the words of misleading critics. The art of an engraving
is discoverable, even by the uninitiated, in the intention
of the lines. You may not have an artist's quickness of
perception, nor his maturer judgment, but if you see an
engraving in which the parts, any of them taken separately, are unintelligible, you will rightly suppose that
the engraver did not know what he was doing, or how to
do it. Art is a designing power. If you can find no
proof of that, reject the work as bad !

*Every line of an engraving ought to have a meaning*, should
be cut in the plate or in the block *with design*. From a
drawing you can erase a false line ; from a metal plate
you can hammer out your faults ; in wood there is no such
easy alteration. On paper or canvas you can rub in a
meaningless background, a formless void, which is all you
may want ; in steel or copper, whether with the graver or
the etching-point, you can cross lines repeatedly so
minutely that all which can be seen is as vague as any
rubbing in. You can not do this on wood. To cut so
finely as to get only colour is next to impossible, and so
far as it can be done useless, for it will not print. It is
for this reason—that every line in wood-engraving bears

I

witness for or against you—that I have spoken of white-line as the true province of engraving in wood.

The best drawings are not made in line. Tints are washed in with a brush, a more rapid and more effective and more painter-like method; and the engraver has to supply the lines, that is to say—he has to draw with his graver such lines as shall represent colour, texture, and form. He is not an artist who neglects one of these; and he is an artist only *so far as every line he cuts has intention of representing something.* In such work he is an artist (though only "copying" the painter or draughts-man) in exactly the same degree in which the translator of poetry is a poet.

Art is not Nature, but, as Emerson well observes, "Nature passed through the alembic of Man." That for the picture. The picture in the engraver's hands passes through a new alembic. It is not a photographic image of the picture: it should not be, but an engraving.

A copper-engraving, which the engraver absolutely draws with his own lines (no drawing at all on the plate except his own), has the dignity of a poetic translation. A wood-engraving from a washed drawing has the same merit. Copper has its pre-eminences, fineness and delicacy. It is folly for the wood-engraver to endeavour to compete on these grounds. But there are brilliant and atmospheric effects, above all, a freshness and painter-like touch, which in copper can not be produced. Especially the character of the painter (not shown in brush-marks) can be rendered in a way not approachable by copper. These are indications of *art* in engraving, the results at which an artist-engraver would aim, and by which alone, according to the degree of his success, he must take rank among artists.

This may fairly lead me to speak again of the qualifications of an engraver. And the first is self-forgetfulness.
Perhaps this is the only ground in which any excellence
can have healthy growth toward perfection. I am sure
that it is the one thing necessary for the engraver, for his
own salvation as well as for the accomplishment of his
work. Only that man will I call artist who can forget
himself in his work. There may be what charity, with
not much precision of speech, will call "art" along with
self-display ; but it will never be art of the greatest. With
such artistic modesty and conscientiousness, a man who
studies what is proper for his work rather than what may
be admired by my few friends this afternoon, and who will
do his best with or without the price he thinks he may
deserve, will, if he have the artist nature, have some fair
chance of success—as an engraver : I do not say as a
transmuter of wood into coin, but as a member of the
great Guild of Art.

For him who would take the way—the only way—of
Art, steep and rugged it may seem, yet not without some
flowers of pleasantness on the roadside, I would fain add
a few truisms (such they appear to me); the repetition of
which at least is harmless.

Self-forgetfulness at his work will not necessitate heed-
lessness of respect for his own manhood. It may be that
some painter or patron may demand his adherence to the
impossible or the undesirable. If it be possible for him
to keep his place as translator rather than to become a
machine in their unknowing hands, let him bear in mind
the duty laid upon every artist to be true to his percep-
tions. There is no other ladder that can reach to
greatness.

Indistinctness is not tone.

A poor engraving may please because the picture is liked for its subject, its sentiment, its effect, or anything else. That is no praise to the engraver.

Do not disdain delicacy, however difficult of attainment in wood, and though you here must be always inferior to your rival in copper. But do not prefer it before force! Combine the two when that can be done with propriety!

Do not be flattered when you are told that "we should not have taken that for wood; we thought it must be steel." A good wood-engraving will not be mistaken for anything else. It should have its own characteristics.

Prefer essentials to non-essentials!

Artifice is not art.

And, to help you to that difficult self-forgetfulness, which should be the last as well as the first thing to be cared for by you,—recollect that an engraver, whoever may employ him, is employed not for his own sake, but for the sake of *the engraving*.

And yet one more word,—only what has been said before in different form. Above all things, as you would be an Artist, worship reverently, and be faithful to the Ideal!

## CHAPTER XII.

### OF WORKS FOR REFERENCE.

**A**FTER so much said in the way of instruction —of what to do and how to do it—I can add but little for the benefit of the student of engraving, except to refer him to a few of the works of our best engravers: making also some running comment, so that, when such works come under his eye he may take full advantage of that farther teaching. The study of one good engraving may help the student more than many words of direction ; and the comparison of various styles will serve to inform his judgment and improve his taste. A list of the most important books containing good examples of our art may also lead to the possession of some : the student knowing what to look for, and what to secure when opportunity may occur.

The works noted below are all to be seen in the library of the British Museum. I give the date of the particular edition to which the paging of my notes refers ; I also give the press-marks by which it will be found in the catalogue.

**118**  **WOOD-ENGRAVING.**

A General History of Quadrupeds, engraved in wood by Thomas Bewick, third edition, 1792. The *Sheep* and *Goats*, especially admirable for variety of texture. In the *Spanish Pointer*, p. 324, observe how, with a few simple lines, Bewick has given a sense of colour. Two tail-pieces, *A Donkey and Children*, p. 16, and *Starved Ewe and Lamb*, p. 59, deserve attention for the snow, well given in both. In the first the sky itself expresses a snowy atmosphere. In the cut at p. 286, *A Fox and Magpies*, the grass and foliage are very rich and vigorous ; the same qualities to be remarked in the *Wolf in a trap*, p. 295. Notice also the *Dog howling in the rain*, p. 305 ; and the *Child pulling a horse's tail*, p. 386,—not a line too much, yet well finished. I would also signalize the cuts at pp. 105, 127, 280, 471. I might point to many more of equal worth, but these may be enough in indication of what is most worth studying. [1256, h. 9.]

A History of British Birds. Vol. I.—Land Birds, 1797. The *Sea-Eagle*, the *Owls*, the *Raven*, the *Greater Spotted Woodpecker*, the *Goatsucker*, and the *Peacock*, may be instanced as of the best (where all are admirable), and will repay most careful study. Bewick's birds are the best work of his own hand. Of the vignette tail-pieces be sure to notice the *Sparrow-Hawk on a spray*, at p. 28 ; a *Dying Dog*,—wet sand and water very cunningly rendered, p. 70 ; *Cow and Magpie*—everything *drawn* with the graver, p. 74 ; " *Esto perpetua* "—observe the snow, the smoke, the wintry branches and thorn hedge, the shadows of the field-furrows, p. 78. Look well, also, at the cuts in pp. 147 and 162— snow again ; at the two *Cocks Fighting*, p. 281 ; at the *Sow* on p. 285 (a dirty subject, but most beautifully engraved) ; the *Dotterel's Feather*, p. 335, &c. &c. [672, g., 17, 18.]

Under the same press-mark will be found, vol. 2,
WATER BIRDS, 1804. The *Tame Duck* is perhaps the very
finest of all Bewick's cuts, both for the bird itself and for
the landscape back-ground : exquisitely drawn (with the
graver) throughout and perfectly finished. The *Velvet
Duck* and the *Scaup Duck* are examples of the use of solid
black. Note also the *Tame Goose*, and the same excellence
of back-ground here as in that of the *Tame Duck*. Of the
tail-pieces, I would select two *fishing subjects*, I think by
Clennell, at pp. 46, 50 ; the *rock and foamy water*, surely
by Clennell, p. 138 ; three *sea-pieces*, again by him, pp.
238, 240, 366. *Two Tramps*, with effect of rain, p. 176,
should not pass unregarded ;˙nor the *Old Woman attacked
by a gander*, p. 303, which Jackson says is Bewick's
own,—a fair presentment, I think, of his general graver-
work ; and worth comparison with the different manner
of work by his pupils in the later *Fables of Æsop*.

The FABLES OF ÆSOP, 1818. This book must not be
confounded (as seems to have been done by Chatto and
Jackson) with the earlier *Fables* by Bewick, of 1779 and
1784. The cuts to the 1779 Fables are beneath an Artist's
notice, only to be cared for by a Collector, who picks up
every thing that has a name ; the *Select Fables* of 1784
have much good work, but little of it can be seen in the
reprints (1820, and more recent), in which the blocks are
worn and battered and have been retouched. This "*Fables
of Æsop*," 1818 and 1823 (it is the better-printed second
edition of 1823 to which I refer you—*Note the exact title
and date!*) is the crowning work of the Bewick School.
Bewick claims the designs, and of course the book was
produced under his direction ; but both drawing and engraving I take to be nearly all by his pupils, the *engraving*

certainly not inferior, but often superior to his own, and mainly, I believe, by Harvey, some perhaps by Nesbit. This one book is of itself almost sufficient for the student. I may point out, as chief examples of most excellent graver-work, the *Wolf, Fox, and Ape;* the *Proud Frog and the Ox;* the *Swallow and other Birds;* the *Lion and the Four Bulls;* the *Old Man and his Sons;* the *Miser and his Treasure* (rich variety of foliage, herbage, rock, and ground); the *Oak and the Reed;* the *Cat and Fox;* the *Bull and Goat* (full of air and light); the *Fox and Boar;* the *Two Frogs;* the *Magpie and Sheep:* marvels of engraving—pictures by incision—white-line graver-work, which can not be too closely studied. Of the tail-pieces, for the same perfection of white-line work, I note among the many excellent the *Man on stilts,* p. 54; *Two Lovers under a hedge,* p. 114; an *Angler,* p. 118; a *Sow and Pigs,* p. 206; the *Cow in a high wind,* p. 214; and " *Waiting for Death,*" p. 338. Nothing can surpass these. The press-mark of the 1823 edition is [12304, f. 12].

RELIGIOUS EMBLEMS, 1809: a series of twenty-one engravings, designed and drawn by John Thurston, the descriptions by the Rev. J. Thomas, under whose name the book must be looked for in the catalogue of the British Museum library. [12304, l. 4.] Notice in the *Soul Encaged,* by Clennell, the grey drapery over the cage, the upper part of the grey figure at the back of the cage, and the daring lines in the figure of Death, and on the rock to the right; in *Wounded in the Mental Eye,* by Nesbit, the light figure in the distance; and the rich bold work in Clennell's *Forest-Feller.* I may also mark as most worthy of commendation Branston's *Rescued from the Floods;* Hole's *Seed Sown; Joyful Retribution, Daughters of Jerusalem, Sinners hiding in the Grave,* and *Awaiting the Dawn,* all by Nesbit; and the *World made Captive,* and *Panting for the Living Waters,* by Clennell. I name so many because they may perhaps be picked up separately. They are all bold, large cuts (the largest five inches by six), and might be called coarse and mannered, but for their very boldness are the better guides for the student; and they have the one great merit—the line is always intelligent and expressive. Thurston probably drew them principally in line, but with leave for the engraver to follow freely and not too mechanically : it is therefore the white line which is everywhere apparent, even in Branston's work. Our frontispiece, a portion of Branston's *Cave of Despair,* will fairly show the character of these fine engravings.

PRACTICAL HINTS ON DECORATIVE PRINTING, by William Savage, 1822 [788. g. 3.], contains this *Cave of Despair* by Branston, and a companion engraving by Nesbit, *Rinaldo and Armida,* from Tasso's *Jerusalem Delivered,* the finest of all Nesbit's works : especially remarkable for his treatment of flesh,—the drapery also good, and the foliage of surpassing richness. The student should look for this, possibly to be met with as a separate print.

And let him also, if he can seize opportunity, obtain sight at the British Museum, or at South Kensington, of Clennell's DIPLOMA OF THE HIGHLAND SOCIETY. At the British Museum (in the Print Room) let him compare this great work with a copy of it by John Thompson, and try by such comparison to learn in what the work by Clennell excels the copy. I can set him no better lesson.

PUCKLE'S CLUB—" The Club, or a grey cap for a green head," by James Puckle, contains some of the best of

Thompson's work, a beautiful frontispiece and other cuts, *Moroso* (the cut on our title-page), *Wiseman, Xantippe,* and *Youth,* of his very best : firm, yet delicate, and rich in line, the foliage in *Moroso* as rich as anything by Nesbit. There are good cuts also by Branston, W. Hughes, H. White, and Mary Byfield, all very characteristic of Thurston's manner.   Pay attention to the freedom of the vignette tail-pieces, due not only to Thurston, but also to the taste of the engravers.   The Museum copy is the second edition, 1834 [8405. bb.].   The frontispiece is wanting in this copy.

BUTLER'S POETICAL REMAINS, a large 4to. [11609. l. 1.], contains the finest portrait ever engraved in wood, by Thompson, after Thurston's drawing ; and some cuts by William Hughes, of his best quality.

Other cuts by Thompson will be found in FAIRFAX'S TASSO: " Godfrey of Bulloigne, or Jerusalem Delivered," 1817 [C. 43, d. 23.].   Notice especially the headings of Books 2, 7, and 13.   And yet a finer engraving by the master-hand (though more in imitation of copper-plate — nothing better of the sort ever done, or to be done) will be seen in WIFFEN'S TASSO, 1826 [2284. 2.], the heading to Book 20.   The other nineteen engravings are by Samuel Williams—excellent all, notably the headings to Books 12 and 15.   Williams' style is peculiarly his own, following neither Bewick nor Branston.   There is much to be admired in his work, yet more in Thompson's ; but go back to the white-line for the best.

NORTHCOTE'S FABLES.—There is a first series, 1828, with good cuts ; but the second series, 1833, is that for the student's examination.   There is only a later edition, 1857, in the Museum Library [12304. d. 26.].   Here more

of tone (though the copy is too heavily printed) will be
found than in earlier works—a greater suavity of line, but
the white-line still in use.   Look at the *Red-breast and
Sparrow*, the *Mole*, the *Young Lady and Pig*, all by Nesbit;
the *Parrot and Singing Birds*, the *Lion, Dog, and Ape*, and
the *Pampered Owlet*, three of Bonner's best work; the
*Poet and Cobwebs*, by Thomas Williams; *Love and Friendship*, by Thompson; the *Peacock and Owl* and the *Delicate
Heron*, by Powis, though with Jackson's name to them;
the tail-pieces to pp. 51, 108, 128, 148, 154, 165.   But we
are already nearing a less masterly time, a time of "finish"
rather than the lines of good drawing; we are losing the
freshness of the older work.

In WALTON'S ANGLER, 1823 [1040. h. 6.], will be found
some fish, deserving close attention : a *Pike*, by Branston;
*Chub, Skegger-Trout, Trout, Salmon, Tench*, and *Pearch*, by
Thompson, all of his own drawing; a beautiful cut also by
him of a *Jar and four fish*, at p. 230; and a good cut by
William Hughes, at p. 142.

The books named above contain the greatest works in
wood-engraving.   Though others might be named, these
are more than sufficient as examples for study.   I might
also refer to later works, of good repute, and good; but I
purposely avoid them, that the student may not be misled
by the more polished and less artistic work there preva-
lent.   In the works I have recommended he will be sure
of the highest teaching, and of learning the essentials of
his art.   The best of wood-engraving was done in the
period here referred to, between 1790 and 1835.   Since
then the artist has given place too much to the mechanic.
I would recall attention to the Old Masters, in some hope
for the restoration of the real art of engraving in wood.

And when the works I have referred to are not acces-
sible, the student may yet find excellent examples in the
works of the old copper-engravers,—bearing in mind the
difference I have emphasized in the two arts, and testing
the worth of all he looks at by the intelligibility and power
of expression in the lines of the same.

# INDEX.

CHISWICK PRESS :—C. WHITTINGHAM AND CO., TOOKS COURT, CHANCERY LANE.